More Memories

and Observations

More Memories

and Observations

of Ted Grove

Order this book online at www.trafford.com
or email orders@trafford.com

Most Trafford titles are also available at major online book retailers.

Note for Librarians: A cataloguing record for this book is available from Library
and Archives Canada at www.collectionscanada.ca/amicus/index-e.html

Printed in Victoria, BC, Canada.

ISBN: 978-1-4251-8607-4 (sc)

*Our mission is to efficiently provide the world's finest, most comprehensive book publishing
service, enabling every author to experience success. To find out how to publish your
book, your way, and have it available worldwide, visit us online at www.trafford.com*

Trafford rev. 8/11/2009

 www.trafford.com

North America & international
toll-free: 1 888 232 4444 (USA & Canada)
phone: 250 383 6864 ♦ fax: 812 355 4082

Contents

PREFACE

I produced my first book of Memoirs in 2006, following the death of my wife, Barbara. I continued to write various narratives because of the pleasure it gave me.

At my present age of just over 89 years, I had no particular urge to produce a second book, but in a compact printed form, I think it is much easier to handle.

The variety of small essays makes it easier for the book to be picked, and laid without the need to remember "the story so far" as required by a novel.

I hope that any reader will find it as pleasing to them, as the pleasure of writing it, has given to me.

TED GROVE

ACKNOWLEDGEMENTS

My family have once again been pleased that I have been able to continue writing various articles as a desirable activity throughout the latter years of my life.

The compositions were transcribed to computer discs by my son Paul. The scripts were proof read, and the final scripts produced. I am grateful to him for his time consuming help.

Introductory Preface

The following pages illustrate a few of the items of play equipment (designed for children, but adults also seem to enjoy them!) which are situated in the **WICKSTEED PARK, KETTERING.** All of them are freely available and the photographs throw a light upon their use in the early decades of the park.

Government legislation in recent years has caused the modification of those considered to be dangerous (Health & Safety Rules) but even in the early years, serious accidents were negligible, although there were, no doubt, a number of bruises and grazes – parental guidance is always desirable!

It can be see that the two people who appear to be flying through the air, are actually both on swings which are on long chains of twisted, linked metal (just visible). I would estimated that their length in those days, were at least 10-12 feet, and the feet of these two, as they stand on the seat of the swings are, at that moment as much as seven or eight yards apart.

The school boy suspended by his arms (right foreground) is about to embark, hand-over-hand, on the rungs of a ladder horizontally suspended about seven or eight feet above the ground.

The lady, dressed in normal clothes of the time (1920's) is flexing her arm muscles on the exercise rings. N.B. The ropes of the maypole on the right of the picture have been <u>temporarily</u> tied high enough to put it out of use).

Another set of exercise rings, showing a school boy, and a man on the left, also a lady (in everyday dress including a brimmed hat which was popular at the time), awaiting her turn on the central ladder and platform.

This form of multi-swing is designed to sway fully to the left and right, with a seating platform moving parallel to the ground. The movement also gives a bouncing action. The two energetic ladies, also in hats and clothes of the time, give both themselves and the two seated passengers an exhilarating time. Note the safety grip guards to ensure they did not slither along the seat. The title of this photograph is shown because the name which this play machine was normally given is the JAZZ.

This is a fast moving see-saw – rather like a swing-boat at the commercial fun fairs, which is pivoted at the top, to allow the platform seat to traverse 90° to the left (from ground level) to 90° to the right thus over 180° half circuit. In this photograph, the male is the energetic activist at one end, whilst at the other end one lady is holding the similar bar at the opposite end, although remaining seated, whilst another passenger is seated on the "pan-seat" and holding on to a similar bar for safety. Note the "grip bars" along the platform seat to accommodate more passengers. Also note the "amazed" look of the onlookers at the back, also the indifference of a disinterested male in the foreground.

N.B. on a couple of occasions I have seen a team of two youths, one at each end, working the swing to the point when one end reaches ground level and one youth would alight from the swing (like dangerously jumping off a moving bus!), and with the next swing movement the second youth would give the final "heave-ho" and the complete platform then swinging over the top to pass through 360°!!

Mr Wicksteed, when made aware of this dangerous action, devised two tapered metal plates in his factory which applied friction together, to slow it down to safe levels. They were fixed near the top of the pivotal point.

Narrative 1

EMBARRASSMENT AND AFTERMATH

I have written about my time in secondary education at the Kettering Central School, and one of the out-of-school activities was the organisation of a troop of Boy Scouts, of which I was a member. Being a co-educational school, the girls were also catered for by the running of a contingent of Girl Guides.

 The leader of the girls' group was a teacher – Miss Latcham, a pleasant (gentle) lady, who taught English and Commerce. She said to me one day – "Ted" (unusual, - boys were normally addressed by their surname) –"The Guides are due to go to a camp shortly, will you be prepared to give up some of your play-time break to help me to get out tents and equipment ready for it?" I was only too willing, and at the time we agreed, I went with her through the girls' playground to the cycle-shed where the camp gear was also stored.

 There were many rolls of tent canvas, bags of tent pegs, cooking equipment, etc., strewn in compact piles and I almost needed mountaineering skills to negotiate them (remember, my boys', not mans' physique). Miss L. selected those she needed and said "I think these should be enough, Ted". At that moment, I was poised with my left foot lodged between two bundles of canvas, whilst my right leg was not long enough to reach the next gap, and I was hampered by a bell tent pole lying at an angle between other bundles. I judged the movement needed to hop from left foot to right and bounded into action – calamity! I did not realise the end of the tent- pole was within inches of my trouser front, and as I made my small jump, the tent pole caught the top of the fly-front of my trousers, and it ripped open the complete row of buttons! (N.B. Zip fasteners were not in general use for trouser fly fronts until about the 1950's) what a plight! Moreover, how could I redeem the situation? As Miss Latcham was standing about a couple of yards away, and the play-ground had at least 50 young ladies with an age range of

11-15, and one or two of 16. I turned my back on them, and as discreetly and nimbly as I could -closed and fastened the middle button to close the gaping front. I still had to traverse the full length of the play area and the girls, and I walked as calmly as I could with one arm draped over my body (the probability was that nobody took the slightest notice of my unusual walk).

I still continued to be regarded in a "teacher's pettish" kind of way, until about a year later, when (being a mixed-sex school) we had one of our weekly lessons in Country dancing (today's pupils may well have looked askance at the study of such a subject) and Miss Latcham also had the responsibility for this subject. During the lessons, the music was switched off to have some particular movement of dance explained "Quiet" said Miss L. but the murmuring continued, including my own "Quiet, Ted", but I still carried on with my subdued expression – until I heard "GROVE!!" That brought my muttering to an abrupt end – the deduction from this was that I was out of favour. So what did I make of this? – I learned a lesson - when in a position of privilege, don't abuse it! I have never forgotten it.

Narrative 2

<u>ASHES TO........OVERFILL!</u>

In days of yore, or more realistically, the days of the declining Victorian era and up to the present time, households were mainly heated by means of an open fire – some older homes still use this method, and a number of the elite set of society have reverted to the open fire, as a feature of their living space. Certainly, in my parent's day, it was our form of heating, and continued with myself during the days after my marriage in 1950.

The daily chore, certainly in the cold days of the late autumn, and winter, also the early days of spring, was the need to clear the ashes from the coal-fire grate, and to re-light a fire the ensuing day. You will realise that, if a very hot fire was left at night, the ashes from it were still very hot, occasionally glowing, thus their removal needed a metal shovel – some people risked wrapping them in newspaper with hazardous consequences – of course, the bins into which they were tipped, were often referred to as ash-boxes, thus the need for them to be made of substantial metal. There was no such luxury as "Wheelie-bins", and the ash men (sometimes called dustmen) needed to be somewhat muscular, and, in fact, this method of collecting was to bring an oval metal bath tin (a kind of hip bath) with a handle at each end. They transferred the ashes/dust etc, from bin to bath tin, then with a mighty swing, heaved it up to their leather-protected shoulder. Now all this is a prelude to a comparison with today's situation.

In the bins of earlier, the majority of the waste consisted of ashes, household dust, old fruit cans, vegetable waste and leftovers of various kinds. Grocery packages were also compressed and thrown in. At the present time, manufacturers of grocery items are very concerned to ensure a "good shelf life", for things which may quickly perish, thus they wrap the product in some kind of paper which can be easily sealed air-tight, but often cover it again with a protective layer, and then a cover on the outside of these with a description of goods, trade name, list of ingredients etc. These covers may not be too bad for small items – biscuits, cakes, etc, but think of the packaging associated with some household goods, - kettles, T.V sets, microwave ovens, irons, etc. The packaging for these certainly needs to be good enough to protect them whilst being handled, hence the liberal use of polystyrene, etc. Its disposal is quite a problem. To put them directly into the wheelie-bin without first breaking it down into small pieces (a job in itself!) would "fill" the bin with considerable air pockets.

The packaging of groceries in earlier days, would, today, raise some eyebrows! I remember going to the shops with my mother, and later, in my late boyhood, actually doing some shopping errands. I give a few examples of packaging of yester-year – potatoes (displayed in barrels) any quantity required – not unlike today, but which are often ready-bagged in suitable quantities using polythene bags. Other common items were dried fruit (currants, raisins, sultanas), which after being weighed, were packed in small, but substantial paper bags, pouched at the bottom, and this allowed it to broaden out into a square shape. No "use-by" dates were necessary – even dried fruit would ooze its residual juice through the paper if left for too long. Similar bags were used for rice, ground rice, flour, sugar etc, but more often the pouched bags were white ones, and it was interesting to see the assistant "bounce" the contents to the bottom of the bags, - fold down the tops, pinch in the top corner and compress them into the body of the bag to make a reasonably firm closed edge. Sides of bacon were hung on display and the choice would be back, cut-through or streaky. The chosen side would be fastened onto a food slicer (early models hand driven) and a thickness gauge set. The cut slices would be wrapped in greaseproof paper. Similarly, the cheese cut by a wire on a marble slab, also in greaseproof paper.

Cooked ham would normally be cut from a cooked whole leg, also in the same way, beef or pork slices. Butter was cut from a huge block, and the shop assistant would weigh the quantity required, and then "patted" into a suitable block, with wooden patting tools – often corrugated to give a fancy surface. Lard was also from a large block, but cut roughly to shape, and again wrapped in greaseproof paper. Potted beef or dripping was cut as required from enamel dishes.

Some of the larger established grocers specialised in coffee beans, roasted and ground – a rich smell if you passed by the shop. Others were tea specialists. Both coffee and tea were packed loose. Biscuits of many varieties were bought loose, and any broken ones were sold separately for a "bargain" price.

Some grocers sold vinegar, using your own bottles, and the same treatment for treacle – more interesting to see it slowly trickling into your own basin.

Today, it is possible to obtain cooked beetroot and pickled onions separately, but it was normally done that way years ago.

Grocers, as well as general stores, sold boiled sweets, usually unwrapped, and slabs of toffee, broken as required by the ha'porth or pen'orth (2 ounces a penny – pre-decimal).

Soap, both toilet and washing – were sold without wrapping. Even the humble toilet roll manufacturers attempted to make the early varieties look attractive by packaging each roll into a separate box!

Christmas fare of nuts, mince pies, chocolates etc was purchased ungarnished.

It take little imagination to realise that if you had one or two customers queuing in front of you, each being served by this extremely slow method, it made shopping even more irksome, and the manufacturers soon hit upon the notion that good, pre-packed, would get more customers through the tills. Hence (today's) packaging and the problems it brings. Fortunately, the recycling of a great deal of wrapping paper is helpful, but the producers need convincing that getting rid of it is tiresome. In spite of this, it is very desirable that we all play our part in sorting the waste. For example, empty cans, can be back as new ones in a matter of weeks, otherwise they would need to be crushed and – buried but where? Landfill sites are getting fewer and fewer, and the only other alternative is incineration – howls of protest from areas where incinerators are planned to be built – certainly a question of overfill!

Narrative 3

A CHAT ON THE PARK

The particular park, about which I would like to share a few thoughts, is known as Rockingham Road Pleasure Park, Kettering. I was born in a house which was no more than a few hundred yards away, thus I have quite a few boyhood sentiments about it.

With the coming of the railway to Kettering in 1857, it brought with it a growing population and a fairly rapid growth in housing. The main spread was taking place northwards, and local Councillors serving the Community at the time, had the foresight to consider that provision ought to be made for recreation space, and the resulting action brought the park idea to fruition, and was opened in 1894. Whilst it is not actually on the Rockingham Road, many of the developing streets and housing complexes evolved with every new road or avenue which sprang up, like side-spurs, from the main Rockingham Road. One of the new side streets was Wood Street, and by the end of the 19th Century, Kettering still maintained a rural feeling. A track which led north-eastwards towards the Weekley Hall Woods was used by people venturing on a country stroll; the track from Wood Street developed into a short road with a line of houses one side, and a field on the other. It became known as Wilson Terrace.

The location of the proposed new park lay a little further northwards, where about ten acres of land was set aside for recreation. The footpath, in fact, ran through the middle of this space. The complete area was enclosed with substantial metal spiked rod fencing. Main double gates were built at each end of the track – always padlocked, unless they were opened for special purposes. A single pedestrian gate was also provided next to the main gates at each end. There were a couple of other pedestrian gates – one on the east side (near the top of Morley Street), and one at the south-eastern corner (leading into Park Avenue). These gates were also padlocked.

In its early years the park was only opened during daylight hours, and a peak-capped Park Keeper was appointed. (In the 1920's, I believe his name was Mr Richards) and he rang a loud hand-bell about half-an-hour before dusk to let the people know that the park would be closed until the beginning of the new day. A house was built for the Park Keeper and family at the south-eastern corner of the park, facing Wilson Terrace.

The length of the track through the park was given a tarmac surface initially, but it was greatly enhanced when a brick-coloured concrete road, with gutters, was laid, and a line of mature trees which grew each side of the road made it an added attraction. The duties of the Park Keeper included the regular mowing of the two bowling greens at the north end, and, if necessary give them a sufficient sprinkling of water to keep them in luxuriant condition.

Further pleasurable activities were installed by the addition of an 18-hole Putting Green, and it was made a little more challenging by the addition of a number of bunker mounds. The green is still in existence as a fenced off portion on the east side of the park, but I understand that, in an effort to maintain interest, the addition of a few "Crazy" golf hazards are now included. In its early days (1920's), I seem to remember that the charge for a game was 3d (old pence), and two putting irons, one golf ball and a score pad were issued.

To maintain the gaming ideas, a giant sized draughts board was laid out, and, using giant draught pieces as big as dinner plates, could be moved over the board by players using a hooked pole to move them. I think they are still in use at stipulated times, and now have a more limited appeal.

The western area of the park contained a drinking fountain with a statuesque metal figure on the top, making it about eight feet in height. A two-level concrete plinth allowed people to reach water taps. They were the press-button kind, and being connected to the water main, meant that pressure on the taps brought forth water, and the waste drained into bowls below them. There were three taps and bowls, and rough cast-iron metal mugs, chained to the fountain. The rims of the mugs were not kind to the lips, but if people were thirsty, and took a chance of sharing the mugs with many other mouths, they may have risked it!

During the First World War, 1914-1918, the park was made available for soldier's use as a temporary depot, by the building of four large army huts on the southern side of the park, and one or two military groups made use of them. Particularly well remembered was the regiment of the Scottish Horse, and a good number of friendships were made. The war also provided a memorial, in the form of a military tank which had been used in battle, as an appreciation of the support and fund raising activities by the people of Kettering. This was placed next to the original large bandstand positioned in about the middle of the park. It was fenced round to keep excitable youngsters and others from using it as a play area. After the war, the army huts continued to be used until about the end of the 1920's or early 1930's, as temporary accommodation for three or four families. At about the same time a new idea for pleasure was conceived – a paddling pool. This was a concrete shallow bowl built on the south-eastern area of the park. It had a diameter of something in the order of 30/40 feet or so – quite a sizeable pool. It was circular and had a surrounding walk-way of about 8 feet in width. A low brick wall made with a wooden flat top, made it possible for Mums (and sometimes Dads) to squat on the wall to watch their offspring paddling and splashing around. Outside the wall a rockery was built, with the rocks interspersed with wild flowers, and other planted flowers to provide a very attractive area. Safe for the youngsters you may say – well! in principle, but no account was taken of the idiotic, unthinking, uncaring people who found their "fun" by throwing cans and bottles (glass and occasionally broken glass) as well as other rubbish into the pool, which brought dire results.

The pool was well conceived and designed, with only shallow depths of water – an inch or so around the edges, with gradual slopes of the bowl to allow the water at no more than a foot depth in the middle. Because of the danger described, a succession of councils ordered the emptying of it, but they continued to allow it to provide a service during school holidays, but it greatly curtailed its usage as compared to its previous availability.

In the preparation of these notes, I have, in the main, relied on my memory recollections on various dates mentioned, and confess that I only thought the pool was in existence for a limited number of years, because of the danger factor, but information I obtained from local history books informed me that the final demolition of the pool did not take place until 1980! In the intervening years, it had a somewhat chequered existence, and the ultimate decision to scrap it, was a very sad day.

The distortion in the gap of time was, no doubt affected by the war years, also my fourteen years living out of Kettering. In a attempt to replace the fun for children, a fairly large wooden, red-painted, mock railway engine was made for a couple of youngsters to play as engine drivers, but it was never of sparkling interest, but new play equipment was added. A few swings, see-saws, and a small roundabout were installed near the south eastern end of the park, and later moved a little closer to the middle of it.

With the advent of the Second World War (1939-45), almost all the heavy spiked railings round the park were dismantled (as were most of the ornamental iron railings in front of dwelling houses). All this metal was sent for use in making military equipment. This meant that the park could never be closed again, and its use, both day and night-time became somewhat debased. A small brick-built, red-tiled roof shelter had been constructed near the centre of the park at the side of the central road. It had bench seats on each of its four sides, to allow people to sit in or out of strong sunshine, and it became a sanctuary for the elderly, particularly the men, sitting, chatting and smoking contentedly. With all the perimeter fencing removed, there came a greater influx of night time activities, particularly the younger generation for "fun and frolics" and part of the "fun" was the apparent pleasure they got in ripping the dividing wooden panels of the shelter. The Council had this repaired many, many times, but enough was enough! – the cost of the regular maintenance, impelled the Council to save the ratepayers from further charges by ordering the demolition of the shelter – another "sad loss"!

The end of the war brought about a few changes. The old large bandstand was replaced by the present one, which was slightly smaller, but very adequate, with sliding wing panels which could be moved as necessary to improve the acoustics also to counter windy conditions to some extent.

During the 1930's the Council arranged regular band

concerts on Sunday afternoons throughout the Spring to Autumn season. Bands were drawn from many towns and village areas, but additionally many renowned national bands – many colliery bands, like the Black Dyke Mills, and other collieries, Foden's Motor Works, Kneller Hall Music Academy, and our own famous Munn and Felton's Works Band, which was formed by the local company in 1932, and by 1935, it had achieved the ultimate accolade of winning the National Annual Brass Band contest. These Sunday concerts were very popular, and crowds of sometimes several hundreds would stand and listen to them. A limited number of chairs were available for the frail and infirm.

The statue fountain was removed and stored away (again because of misuse). In later years when an area in the Horsemarket was being developed, local enthusiasts requested, and were granted permission for the statue/fountain to be erected in this area near the top of Market Street, albeit without the water and drinking facility. It was given a paint up-lift, and it made an attractive addition to this area.

The old First World War tank was removed and the army huts were dismantled, as families were re-housed. These alterations could be counted as an improvement for the park, but the post Second World War brought some deteriorations. There were public toilets at the north end of the park, screened to some extent by trees and bushes. These became tarnished by it being used by drug takers, also some sexual activity which brought about the demise of the facility. New secure individual toilets were later installed.

On the town's annual Carnival Day the park became the dispersal point for all the contestants. Up to 1948 funds received went to the benefit of the local Hospital, but after it became funded by the government in 1948, funds thereafter benefited the blind people of the population. To end these carnival days, a big variety of stalls, games, demonstrations, competitions etc, continued in the carnival atmosphere.

When I was a boy (in the 1920's) our excitement was kindled when, occasionally we watched a horse-drawn, three-gang mower, cutting off the tufty grass. The tufts were left on the ground, and if it was dry enough, quite a heap of grass cuttings would be built up, and played with, handfuls being thrown at each other. On reflection, we did not understand the damage of germs from dog-mess. Even today, when owners are required to "clean up the soilage", there are still stray dogs roaming the streets and the park, with no responsible owners.

In spite of the many passing problems, the park still serves its purpose as a leisure space; it remains popular in Spring, Summer and Autumn seasons (and for the "braves" in Winter) to allow people to take gentle exercise, and to breathe good air. I have been unable to visit it of recent years, due to my age and difficulty of movement, so I have had to rely on my past memories. As already mentioned, exact dates are uncertain, but I have put them in some logical sequence, which should make it a semblance of being a fairly true record.

I think in closing, we ought to praise the thoughts of past councillors who considered the desirability making leisure a factor of our lives. It is also to be hoped that people seeking their own fun, do not impede the needs of other people!

Narrative 4

KNIVES AND FIREARMS ON THE STREET

This has been a growing problem over the past decade or so and has, today, reached serious levels.

No doubt many brains have been engaged to contain the problem, but success rates have not been good enough to date. The campaign to have knives, guns and other destructive weapons surrendered under an amnesty, brought results of a large quantity being handed in, but there must be far too many still in existence, and the sale of new ones is still at too high a level!

Many people will have their own ideas of what ways the situation might be improved. My own thoughts, which I now commit to paper, may possibly be worth pursuing. You may, or may not consider my suggestion, but it would, of course, need much deeper examination and thought.

Introduction – instead of meting out initial punishment through the Courts, I believe the following procedure to be worth a thought.

Anyone caught by any correctly applied apprehension who is found to be carrying any destructive missiles, would immediately have them confiscated. Instead of an immediate Court procedure, they would be cautioned, and required to give their name and address, also the name and location of parents/partners, or those responsible for their care. NB to ensure that these details are correct (by a later check if necessary), an on-the-spot set of fingerprints be taken and these to be held for a limited period only; say five years, but, if considered desirable, up to the age of 18 years.

In place of Court jurisdiction, the punishment would be for their name and details to be listed on a central national register. In view of a doubtful track record of some government's installation of specialised computers, I would not envisage the setting up of some grandiose Government department, but a small competent staff, using a <u>standard</u> computer system, building up an alphabetical list, given an identity number, and to which <u>all</u> police forces quickly send details of those apprehended. If, at a later date, any of these people are arrested for <u>actually using</u> knives or other missiles, any sentence made by a judge, to be doubled. If these persons are apprehended on a second occasion after having previously been cautioned, the sentence to be <u>trebled</u>; if caught for a third time for <u>carrying</u> the arms after previous cautions, the sentence increased to a greater degree.

There is just a chance that this threat held against them <u>may</u> have the effect of curbing their thoughts before committing the greater crime.

- Just a germ of an idea!

Narrative 5

A FADED DREAM

Old parts of Kettering served the people well enough – tracks, footpaths, workshops, sheds etc, but as the town developed, some of these older area were left behind. For example the main shopping thoroughfares developed from High Street, Gold Street, and limited growth into Newland Street, Silver Street and Montagu Street, which (it seems to me) left some areas under used. I would not describe them as derelict because, due to my age and infirmity, I have not seen them for many years, and thus I cannot be sure of the present state of these areas.

One such space – once containing such enterprises as the 'Evening Telegraph' press and offices, a footwear warehouse, a group doctors' surgery, and a government office, among other undertakings. As these left, not a lot took their places, although I understand there has been some dwellings built.

My dream has been to develop the whole of this area, bounded by Gold Street, Silver Street, Dalkeith Place, Market Street, and High Street. By the introduction of a new addition to the town centre shops, particularly encouraging the individual traders who wish to start small, but grow larger. I visualised the whole area would need a two lane ring road, first to the rear of the main centre shops, with the entrance to, and exit from it near to the top of Market Street. This would serve for the delivery of goods to new businesses, and, incidentally afford deliveries to the established shops. It would also allow small delivery vans for the smaller traders.

I would name this area the "Gold Star" Shopping Precinct. Access for pedestrians to be made by walkways of suitable widths, say, six to 12 feet depending on anticipated numbers of people using them. Possible access areas such as from Gold Street – using, and (widening if possible) the present walk through to the old 'Ivy's Café' of past years. Another at the north end of High Street – at present a rough track leading to Dalkeith Place. A third one, using Dryland Street, and a fourth one from Market Street – using the access, which, years ago, led to an electrical trader,(probably about halfway between High Street and London Road). Each of these walkway entrances clearly indicated by a Gold Star logo (probably on a coloured curved small scroll over each entrance) to have crossings so as to negotiate the two lane ring road for safety reasons, with clear warnings on both the road and the walk ways.

The construction of suitable shop units, to be built in a series of blocks of (say) two small "starter" shops and one medium sized one, - another may be two medium sized ones etc, and these built within the ring road, set back sufficiently for safety reasons, and as many units as could be accommodated within the service road. Because the slope on the central area being fairly pronounced, those built on the lower part could be with an extra storey. The shop frontages would all face inward toward the area where shoppers circulate.

I visualise that the shop units would each have a top storey as living quarters, for the owners, or staff, or other selected tenants. If the top floor dwelling had the floor extended at their rear (by adequate girders) this would form a kind of bay for traders' vans, and staff cars. With people living 'over the shop' it may discourage vandalism!

The main ring road would need to have suitable fire hydrants at strategic intervals, and adequate drainage/sewerage to the nearest and most suitable connection to the mains. Traders display windows and fascia name signs directed to "catch the eye" of those people who may be judging and buying from the new shops.

If such a development as this could ever be contemplated, I firmly believe it should remain under local authority control, with a precinct manager and small staff, and NOT a developer. I say this because a developer would set rentals to as high a level as possible (a lethal blow for young traders trying to get started). An "E.T." report published at the time I was writing these notes (approx. July 19th & 20th) stated that a trader had quit the town centre because of the high rents charged! My own feeling is that rents for a new unestablished business should be at least 20% to 25% less than those of established firms, with regular reviews at one, two or three years intervals – increases based on increased trade.

The mix of shops would be very important to offer good choice. I think a cafeteria is desirable for morning coffee, lunchtime snacks, and afternoon teas, and any other enterprising ideas. I would exclude charity shops (important though they may be!) also such companies as estate agents, insurance companies etc. This new zone must offer something different and vibrant!

Ideally some roof covering would be an asset as a protection against heavy rain/snow etc. As mentioned, I was informed there has been some housing development, and should any kind of initiative be contemplated, it may be desirable to plan part of it for shops. It would take much thought and discussion to bring in new ideas, also the strength of resolution among councillors, would, of course, be vital.

A Faded Dream?? – probably, but with discussion and resolve it could turn the Kettering Centre into a good traditional shopping area, a blossoming one, in fact a rather unique creation. Perhaps even only half a centre! Ah well!

Narrative 6

TOP OF NORTHALL!

The title of this story is the often quoted description of an interesting region of Kettering which, during the early growth of the town, Northall Street to give it its full title, became a branch road at the south end of Rockingham Road. Whilst it did not form part of the town's shopping area, it became a busy link westwards to join the country's main road for traffic moving south and north (designated as the A6).

As local traffic at the time of its first appearance consisted of a scattered mixture of horse and carts, cycle, and pedestrians, the width of this narrow road, served its purpose. Nevertheless, the top area of this junction had quite a few shops and public houses. The two main corner shops were Blackett's Wine and Spirit shop on the north-east corner and next to it northwards along the Rockingham Road was The Hare and Hounds, and The Vine public houses. On the south east corner was Eastman's the butcher, and there was a small line of shops – general stores, etc, and a cobbler's shop (Holland's); a little below these was The Robin Hood public house. Just beyond that, Northall Street divided with a gentle curve to the left – this road led to Tanner's Lane, passing Lindrea's leather factory, and a corrugated metal hall, formerly a billiard saloon and later used by the British Legion Association, the road again divided to the right into Tanner's Lane. The opposite side of this link road contained an area where the local Co-operative Society Hall was situated, and this was used until the impressive Central Hall was opened in Montagu Street in 1930. Without offering any further description, the road continued on through the old Post Office Arcade and into Gold Street.

From Blackett's corner shop, travelling westwards was the prosperous business of Jack Cross (Senior) which was a wholesale newspaper distributor that supplied other shops in the town and outlying areas. Jack also maintained a busy general shop, described as the Central Bookshop, and the Central Printing Works, which was next door, and just behind the shop. Jack's son (also Jack) became involved in the businesses, and he and his equally hardworking mother developed the enterprise greatly.

The outlook from Jack's shop was fairly open and on the right side was the old day school – St. Andrew's. On the triangular area formed by the school's frontage and the Northall Street/Tanner's Lane junction, became the focus of an unusual gawky structure built of large sheets of cast iron. These were erected into a circular shape to surround an area of about 12 or 13 feet diameter. Two openings were left as entrances and curved screens were set a few feet inside each opening, and these provided a degree of privacy. The complete circular building had a gentle curved roof shaped up to its pinnacle – the whole building resembled the shape of a small bandstand! It was painted in a dull dark sage green colour. What on earth was the need for such a place? Well, the local council at the time of its inception, (late 19th Century) decided that men required the facility of a urinal – not the ladies who, it seems, appeared to have no need for such a place. Now, if I mention the name <u>CLOCHMERLE</u>, some of the older generation may vaguely remember in the early decades of television programmes that this was the title given to a story set in the Low Countries (Belgium, Netherlands, and Luxembourg) about just such a building.

The complete tale revolved around the townsfolk of a small population in one of these countries, being completely divided in their opinions of whether such a similar toilet facility (almost an identical building to the Kettering one) should, or should not agree to its destruction. In the case of the one in our own town, no such choice was even considered. Around 1929/30, the urinal (which, whilst regularly cleaned, was odorous and unhygienic) was declared to be unfit, and was demolished, to be replaced by an underground facility – still as a urinal only, - still for men only, but being automatically flushed, provided a healthier service. This, together with Jack Cross's shop and printing works, plus all the other buildings at the "top of Northall" received a death-blow to give rise to the much widened thoroughfare, and this was around the mid 1970's – Faded memories remain!

Narrative 7

A DAY-DREAM TOO LATE!

It is always easier, with hindsight, to make more judicious decisions about circumstances as they arise. In this particular narrative, it is certainly too <u>late</u> to change anything, but I want to fantasise on what <u>could</u> have been a different, and an alternative also, (only in my opinion) a more attractive development of the Newlands Centre complex in Kettering.

     In 1931, Dalkeith Place was opened up to become a more spacious shopping area, by the demolition of the Methodist Church (rebuilt as the Central Methodist Church in School Lane) and this allowed the widening of the, then, narrow Silver Street. This was completed in 1932, and accepted by most people as a desirable improvement. At the time, it was also intimated that the narrow Newland Street would, in due course, be given similar treatment. Unfortunately, the 1939-45 war, left the country few funds for this sort of development, and it was given no priority. Towards the end of the 1960's, attention was again focussed on the town centre development, and this resulted in developers eradicating a great deal of the existing buildings in Gold Street, Newland Street, and properties bounded by Tanner's Lane and Lower Street.

     At that particular time in history, many developers, when given a project to undertake, seemed to prefer commencing with a complete open space, with no regard as to whether existing properties could be incorporated as part of the plan, thus anything of <u>possible</u> historical interest, (such as Gold Street's Victorian architecture, and the much older, stone built premises of the old Grammar School) were obliterated. Many people regarded this with regret, and, since Gold Street was one of the main roads for shopping, it was also considered desirable for the main entrance to the new projected Newlands (initially Newborough) Centre.

     My fantasy was that I looked at this from a <u>completely</u>

different angle, and I would have liked to have seen the <u>widening</u> of Newland Street, as previously projected, and the <u>main</u> entrance to the Newlands Centre would have been in Newland Street. The Victorian shop fronts of Gold Street would have been retained, with the ghastly cream painted frontage of one of the shops removed, leaving the original red brick and the stonework still as part of any new development. I would have retained the Post Office Arcade, and made that as the entrance into a new <u>undercover arcade</u>, with new shops on both sides, and stretching out as far as Tanner's Lane and even up to Northall Street. This would have made an <u>excellent addition</u> to town centre shops. I would have retained the inscription on the Gold Street stone arch, but re-named the Arcade with something like "Mailer's Arcade", or similar. From these new shops, access would be made to all shops developed from the widened Newland Street (right side of the Arcade), and to shops on the Lower Street on the other side.

If Newland Street was considered (as at present) as a traffic free road, it could have still been so, but the widened street could have been developed into a pleasant shopping area, by the provision of a series of neat flower beds down the centre – a very agreeable view.

One other thought – the "island" of shops, known as Bakehouse Hill, contained some <u>thriving</u> retailers, but I imagine it was declared "due for development" and once this is announced, owners and/or retailers would no <u>longer be interested in maintaining their properties</u>, because, (they would reason), why should they spend money on buildings which will be demolished? In other words, it becomes a "twilight zone", which, over a few decades slides into a state of being <u>completely run down</u>. The same happened when old Northall Street also Queen Street properties were declared as due for development. I am not certain of the state of the properties on the Bakehouse Hill triangle, but if it could have been retained, it would still have been part of the thriving retailers of the town. It would also have been further improved if the last two or three shops at the bottom of Gold Street were to have been built with a greatly <u>curved</u> corner, which I think would have looked more presentable than box-like corners. Consider the present main shopping streets of Kettering – Gold Street, High Street, Dalkeith Place, Lower

Street, etc, - these mostly have gently undulating curves, and any newcomers to the town would find themselves taken by surprise around each new bend, to discover a plethora of renowned traders which can be found in other large towns and cities mostly in the same long straight rows.

As I gave, in the title of this account – "too late", I still wished to put this fantasy into words to "get it off my chest", although I am possibly the only one who thinks it a good idea!

One last thought on "historical" buildings – Kettering's old buildings such as the Victorian shop fronts, Beech House, the old Grammar School etc. if they were still standing, they would be gently moving towards being a historical heritage, as were the ancient buildings in such places as Chester, York etc. Succeeding generations would look upon them as "historical" in due time. It would be ludicrous to think that Councillors in Chester would agree to any of their ancient properties being demolished because they are too old!

Narrative 8

PROUD AS A PEACOCK

I have used the peacock title to this jotting because there are a few things I would like to say about pride!

My own view is that people can feel a degree of pride in some success that they have achieved through their own efforts. Assessing a particular task and working to achieve it, would give one a "flush of success", when completed. At the same time I have some reservations.

There are degrees of pride that can reach such levels which, in my opinion, are unacceptable. It can become overwhelmingly intolerable if it extends to a person becoming haughty – it is sometimes referred to as "giving oneself airs". Other phrases which come to mind are, "getting on your high horse", being "puffed up", arrogance, vanity, self praise, swollen headed, to glory in some situations and a number of other descriptions. Without being labelled with any of these patterns of behaviour, I am sure that a person having personal pride in their appearance, cleanliness, general bearing, ability to relate to others, etc, is more than justified.

Anyone who gets engrossed in pride, can fall into another scurrilous state of mind – that of boasting. Think of some of the ways that this can be expressed – bragging, gloating, swanking, swollen headed, vaunting, too big for their boots, bombastic, blowing own trumpet, chauvinism, shooting a line, self importance and others. I am not sure whether anyone who makes a habit of boasting would wish to be "tarred with such brushes". If they don't mind it, they will continue strutting through life with a "very thick skin", as many of their fellow citizens' look on them with contempt.

To sum up – allow pride to reach levels which give one a boost, but always consider the importance of keeping it well under control. People, in general, relate more easily with those who do not believe themselves as being of a superior class!

TAILPIECE

A line extracted from a well-revered hymn – "Forbid it, Lord, that I should boast" (from "When I survey the wondrous cross")

Narrative 9

HEY! WHAT'S YOUR GAME?

I chose this unusual title because I want to examine the significance of it to our lifestyle. As babies in our prams, we are introduced to a number of ways to develop activities which are much more than feeding, sleeping, bathing etc, (all of these are necessities). At the same time, most parents consider it to be important to introduce their children to the more <u>sensual</u> pattern of living – sound, sight, touch, particularly their close contact with their parents and others. Most parents (very often more likely the mother) spend a great deal of a child's waking hours talking, whispering, smiling softly singing, etc, to encourage the baby to respond – all extremely important! To assist parents to increase the intensity of these actions, they make use of toys of various sorts – cuddly toys (tactile) squeaky and "talking" toys (sound) rattles, balls etc. The "surprise" aspect bone teething rings and similar articles (to encourage gripping, holding etc.), mobiles on cots/prams etc, (to encourage vision), bath time toys, etc, (indicates ability to float in water), the soft <u>real</u> sponge (gives the child another touch/squeeze experience).

At a little later age, an introduction to books (soft linen pages) to illustrate pictures, words, stories, etc, and the importance of reading, and as they get older, to make marks with crayons and pencils to establish the link between writing and reading. (It can be seen at this stage, that those who become parents at a very young age ought to be educated enough to realise the importance of what parenting is about!) As they increase in age, introduction to playgroups, combines the process with the additional activities of dancing/singing ("ring 'o' roses", "Mulberry Bush" and so on), parents continue to keep up "action games" with the likes of "Pat-a cake", "Leg over leg", "Gallopy gallopy" and others.

At infant school, exercises are made in the form of group

games (which, in my boyhood) included egg and spoon races, games with beanbags, potato races, etc.

At home, games could include such things as draughts, halma, lotto, dominoes, card games like "Snap", "Happy Families", "Kanugo & Lexicon", (both simple "Scrabble" kind of games).

Further increase in age brings in the more intricate toys – Meccano, Lego, Bagatelle, Toy Cinematograph, simple cameras (box, folding etc.), before the media development of camera/ mobiles, also in earlier times, slide projectors.

Street games (when streets were safe!) such as "catty" (involving action, judgement and calculation) "release", "tick, you're it", "leap frog", "skipping" and "hop scotch", "whip and top" (all mainly energetic). More sedate games such as marbles, five-stones, collecting (uniform badges & buttons or other items found to hold an interest) also metal puzzles and a variety of others.

At school, there are lessons in physical education, sporting games – running, jumping, hurdles and team games like football, tennis, netball, and cricket. Lessons also in Art, Drama, and debating and so on.

The modern generation have been introduced to an enormous influx of micro-technology, calculators, mobiles, and computers bringing about their <u>mass</u> of games, as well as the game shows on TV. Many activities undertaken in earlier times included hiking (a <u>mass</u> uptake in the 1930's!) Spelling "bees" (very popular), quiz games, darts, (individual and team). Clubs and Societies of various kinds arrange a multitude of activities, whilst professional companies cater for mass gymnasia sessions. Enthusiasts can purchase their own gym equipment for use at home.

Now in reviewing this brief list of various games, I have only included those which I have either experienced, or I know a little about them. It is by <u>no means</u> a complete list, in fact, different areas of the country have their own "home produced" games.

I thought about the kinds of activities which are prevalent with today's modern people, and I get the impression that a great deal of their time is spent with <u>modern</u> equipment which causes them to sit for many hours, staring at a computer screen using the multifarious selection of games involving destroying, capturing, shooting etc., of some fictitious alien. This may well speed up their responses in a situation, but it does not provide much <u>physical</u> activity. Should this matter? – As I write this essay (August 2006) it has been announced that many children are becoming overweight – obese is the word they use. In fact obesity, it is said is <u>as great a problem</u> as those who are undernourished – India and China (both fast developing countries) come into this category because more of their population is now being <u>overfed</u>! (Actual statistics – 1 billion overfed and 800 million undernourished) countries like our own, the USA and a number of European countries add to this problem.

There are many reasons for being obese, but I am not an expert who can fully explain it, however I well remember the days after the end of the 39/45 war, that some mothers bottle-fed their children using National Dried Milk, and it was said that, in a lot of cases, children were becoming overweight because of it, but as I said, I can only refer to what the professionals tell us. One thing which is repeatedly dwelt upon is that few people, particularly in their young days (which sets a pattern for their future life), pursue <u>active</u> exercise! Well if a comparison is made between the games we play today, and when we were young, with those which seem to take preference at the late childhood/teenage stage, most of the recently developed activities, do not do much to "tone-up" the body, and, the experts tell us, that this allows muscles to slacken and become flabby. So I repeat, "What is <u>your</u> game?" – Good health to everyone!

Narrative 10

JUST RELAX! (PART 1)

The growth of Kettering quickened after the coming of the main line railway in 1857. The population increased as industries such as clothing, engineering and boots and shoes expanded.

Work in factories was quite intense, and at the end of the working day, people began to look for ways in which they could "wind down". A lot turned to alcohol drinking, and two main hotels – "The Royal" and "The George" catered for those of the so-called elite classes. Working men organised themselves into "clubs", where, for a small subscription, they could enjoy their drinking at more favourable prices, because they were not set up for the purpose of making a profit. There was also an alcohol-free hotel – "The Albion", but this eventually closed.

People sought a variety of ways by which they could be entertained, and it gave rise to the introduction of small dramatic groups. By the early 20th Century, an Operatic Society was established, and in Kettering, they performed, non-professionally, some of the musical presentations which were being professionally offered in London and other larger cities. I personally remember some of the shows presented locally, such as "No, No, Nanette", "Desert Song", "Maid of the Mountains", etc. Even today, we hear music from them, e.g. "Tea for Two" (from No, No, Nanette).

By the early 20th Century, another form of entertainment appeared - "moving pictures". The earliest of these in Kettering was set up in the old Corn Exchange on the market place by a Mr. Vint, and gave it the name of Vint's Electric Palace. Early films were produced on celluloid film strip, and the nature of this material was that it was very brittle, also the constant passing of the film through numerous projectors, had the effect of building up many fine hair-line scratches on the surface of the film which made the picture projected on to the screen to be in a constant heavy rain, and almost obliterated the picture! The brittle nature of the film also caused quite a number of sudden break-downs!

By about 1905, Mr.Vint had left the scene, and for almost the next decade another proprietor changed the name of the cinema to the Hippodrome. In 1913, the first purpose-built cinema, - the Electric Pavilion, - was opened in the High Street, and whilst the projection improved, the films were still "silent", also the very occasional breakdown, but it superseded the Hippodrome which ceased to function.

The 1920's heralded the very rapid growth of cinemas throughout the country, and after the end of the First World War (1914-18), another small purpose-built cinema opened in Eskdaill Street, and was known as the "Empire". Kettering also had two theatres – the Victoria Hall and the Colisseum. The former was used for public functions of all kinds, as well as theatrical productions, and the Colisseum catered for all kinds of variety shows.

With the rapid development of television from the mid to late 1950's, it caused theatres throughout the country to become less viable, and both became cinemas, as an economic necessity. The Colisseum suffered a serious fire in the 1930's, and its proprietor, Mr Sherwood, had it rebuilt,, still as a theatre, and it was renamed "The Savoy".

The Pavilion (later became "The Gaumont"), also the "Victoria Picture House", were made more impressive because they both employed commissionaires at their front entrance. The Pavilion's man was attired in a long length navy, double-breasted coat, also wearing a peaked cap, and both were enhanced by red and gold braid. The Victoria's man was similarly dressed, but basically coloured medium brown. Both presented imposing attendants. The Victoria later became the Odeon in 1936.

In 1935, another new cinema was built, with its architecture of a more modern style, and whilst it did not employ a commissionaire, the manager himself – Mr. Morley-Clarke, regularly graced the large foyer in evening dress (bow-tie and tails), which appeared to be a more grandiose welcome to patrons. It was named "The Regal" until it was taken over by the Granada group, and renamed accordingly. Under this management, The Granada not only showed films, but also ran celebrity concerts of many big bands of the time like Ambrose,

Jack Jackson, Roy Fox, Nat Gonella and many more. It also changed to reflect the new mood of the 1960's, by organising presentation of some of the big names of that time – a few examples – the "early" Rolling Stones, Adam Faith, Dusty Springfield, Marianne Faithfull, The Searchers, The Tremeloes and many others! It became the "Gala" in the 1970's, and catered for bingo fans.

So for many years Kettering(after the demise of the Hippodrome) had five cinemas, which were regularly bolstered by a mass of customers, often long queues waiting. As they often had two performances each week (Mon, Tues, Wed, and Thurs, Fri and Sat) they gave the public a wide choice, - if they could afford it! Even though the pre-decimal prices charged by the cinemas ranged from 3d, 6d, 9d, and 1/-, and later up to 2/6d.

In their final years, they all closed, and the last one (The Savoy) was re-named the Ohio, and were superseded by a multi-screen cinema the new Odeon.

In its early days, I remember the Pavilion was the first Kettering cinema to try out a "talking" picture. It was very primitive, as an operator was employed to keep the gramophone synchronised with the picture on the screen, and quite often the sound occurred a fraction of a second after an actor's mouth movement. Incidentally, this first "sound" film, was almost the first in "colour" shown in Kettering.

The first professionally installed sound equipment was in the Victoria "Picture House" (as described itself on the front canopy over the entrance). It was the Western Electric Sound System, but in the first few years, all "talkies" were addressed as 50%-75% talkie, until they all became 100% talkies.

In their early days, cinemas ran two distinct "houses" for their programmes, but later they all ran as continuous performances.

Narrative 11

<u>JUST RELAX! (PART 2)</u>

In Part 1, I described in the main, the world of the cinemas, although The Savoy and The Granada used their stage facilities for professional acts as well as the local groups. For one or two years The Savoy (by arrangement with the Northampton Repertory Theatre Company) presented plays by the Rep.Company.

Another theatre was also created when the Kettering Technical College (later Tresham Institute) used the large examination hall, by incorporating a stage, fly tower and dressing rooms at its eastern end, and a retractable tiered seating provided a kind of a slightly raised balcony. It was named The McKinlay, after the then Principal of the College. Sadly this is due for demolition by the year 2007. An alternative one is planned at the Kettering Leisure Park to be opened by the end of 2007 (if there are no hitches). The McKinlay and The Savoy were much used by the local dramatic societies for their very professional style productions.

Kettering has been well-blessed by The Operatic Society, The Theatrical Society, and they have been supported at times by such groups as The Cytringan Players, Gilbert & Sullivan Society, United Theatre Group, and others.

Another "plus" for Kettering has been the considerable interest in The Kettering Choral Society, The Seagrave Singers (continued, with a name change from The Cavendish Singers out of respect caused by the untimely death of the late Muriel Wallis, who founded The Cavendish Singers). At one time there was also a Chamber Choir. A regular Kettering Eisteddfod draws together many musical talents.

On the question of other forms of relaxing activities, interest was always shown in the ballroom style dances. Again, this town had quite a number of semi professional bands. I cannot recall them all, but prominent names were The Richardson Players, Collegions,

The Centralians (of which I was the drummer), Tom Ashby and The Rhythm Aces. All of these bands had from 5 to 8 players. There were many others of a smaller size, 3 or 4 players pre-1939-45. The bands often ran their regular public dances, but also provided music for many well known occasions, Burn's Night, NALGO Social Club, St. David's Night, etc as well as many private functions.

In the 1960's, huge changes were brought about when pressures from the younger generations in the U.S.A. (San Francisco) advocated "love" not "war" style of life, with the help of drugs, also a more casual approach of sexual fraternisation. Society is experiencing the consequences of this with a frightening growth of sexual diseases – a much "too liberal" style of relaxation! (in my opinion).

Part of this social change brought together mass gatherings of young people, and their music and dancing style changed accordingly. First London and the big cities, but not long afterwards towns of Kettering's size. Gone were the gentile movements of the established dance halls and a "honey-pot" of such activity became associated with a place known as the "Tin Hat". This was the nickname given to a Working Men's Club - The Athletic Club – associated with the Kettering Town Football Club (-"The Poppies"), so that their spectators could have "refreshments" available at the matches. The building itself comprised a fair sized construction made from corrugated sheet metal. The interior had no great elegance, but the frolicking masses took little notice of their surroundings. It drew crowds from a wide radius around Kettering, and, of course, there were occasional brawls, no doubt because of alcohol. The mode of dancing was no longer a gentle holding of partners, but to be a few feet away from each other, with their bodies gyrating and arms moving in all directions. Well, if that's what they want! – all a kind of uncontrolled relaxation.

Many Working Men's Clubs gained trade sponsoring this kind of dancing, by organising such events. On the other hand, many elderly people enjoyed (and still do) the old style dancing, and hold regular sessions of it.

During the 1930's, there were quite a few Schools of Dancing, which taught both stage and ballroom modes – quite popular.

Narrative 12

JUST RELAX! (PART 3)

As well as the cinemas and theatres and dancing, there was a host of other activities organised by various churches, societies and clubs, covering a variety of both large and smaller groups which catered for people's needs, and many of them still exist.

I list examples – most are self-explanatory, by their name, but I will add any odd additional thoughts as I list them.

Cycling (both leisure and competitive), - rambling (once referred to as hiking); debating; gramophone; poetry and reading (local members contributed as well as those recognised nationally); whist drives; bridge clubs; darts; skittles; coffee mornings; tea dances; quiz groups; car rallies; tuition of music; (all instruments and voices), - education.(such as Open University); Keep Fit; (gymnasia and own home); D.I.Y. repairs (and other talents); rowing; photography; amateur dramatics; choral groups; Bible study; art clubs; lunch clubs; model making; preservation groups; thoughts on civic development; play groups for children; amateur sports (football, rugby, tennis, cricket); St. John's and Red Cross work; leaders (for youth groups); scouts; guides; cubs; Boy's Brigade; etc); Harriers, fishing, knitting, crocheting.

I am sure there must be quite a few others, but you will see that many of them need some kind of physical activity – even this is a form of relaxation, - a change from normal routine.

In addition to the list, there were, and still are, people who provide entertainment for others – purely on a voluntary basis. In my early days, we had individuals and small groups performing at social functions – Billy Cox playing his accordion. Leslie Law and his accordion band – Leslie also taught pupils. – Two local brothers (the Sadlers) performed as a duo, Ray, the pianist, with brother Arthur, with amusing and entertaining songs, some of them written by themselves. I also remember a trio of old songster similarly performing old-fashioned and comical songs such as "Dandelion, Daisy and Daffodil".

Today, a group calling themselves the "Variations" perform a programme of songs and sketches.

I cannot imagine that many people today, particularly the young ones, would wish to "stir away" from their computer games, (and this is not to be condemned out of hand!) but this excludes all other possible activities mentioned, and this <u>limits</u> the relaxation element, because the computer style of action will need a great deal of focussed concentration. Remember the saying – "a change is as good as a rest". I think that may be a fair statement.

Narrative 13

A GYM SLIP-UP

Elsewhere in my various essays, I have said that my time in secondary education was spent in a co-educational school – the Kettering Central School. It enrolled pupils who showed an academic attitude, although the most promising of whom were directed to the single sex, Grammar School for boys and the High School for girls.

The Central School selected those with a similar potential, and was limited to an annual intake of two classes of about 35 pupils, and as it was required that those attending it stayed for a four year course, the total school population was around 300 which included a few staying on for a short period. It had a teaching staff of ten.

Part of the curriculum set aside one period of about one hour per week for what was briefly described as P.T. (Physical Training) – this was later changed to P.E. (Physical Education). There were also times set aside for games – football and cricket for the boys, and hockey and netball for the girls. Because it was not a large school, it did not have a purpose-built gymnasium, and as the P.T. lesson occurred, it was either done on the school playground or, if the weather was inclement, in the school's main hall. Because of the size of the staff, there was no specially appointed teacher, and it fell to one of the male staff to take the lesson for boys, and a female member for the girls. I think it must have been the case of selecting the younger and probably the fittest member to do it.

The occasion I will now describe was where the two classes of first year girls, which is just over 30 pupils, were required to do their class in the school hall. The lady teacher, whom I will describe as Miss. X, took on the teaching role, and I would describe Miss. X as a feisty lady. (I use the dictionary definition of this as someone who is <u>excitable,</u> and has a strong <u>personality</u>). I am, of course, uncertain of the instructions she gave to the girls, but she must have instructed them to "take off your gymslips!" I can only imagine the reaction of the girls, because the main hall had classrooms all around it, and as the lesson times changed, so both boys and girls moved from one classroom to another, this, at the time the girls appeared "ready for action" they, no doubt felt very embarrassed at "being on show!" wearing a white tunic top blouse, black knickers and black stockings – all perfectly decent (by today's standards!)

I can only assume that Miss X, hearing the lament of the girls to disrobe, set an example by removing her own day dress beneath which, she wore a short, pale green silky under slip. The immediate effect was surprising but - (repel the thought!), extending a little below the slip revealed the bottom of the elasticised leg of D.K's (I presume!) D.K's?? – the correct name is <u>Directoire Knickers</u>. One might ask how I should know about such garments. For the single reason, that during my 23 years in the manufacturing industry, I was employed for about 8 of them with a company which manufactured ladies' lingerie, - about two years as the Production Manager, and just over two years as the Sales Manager. This, now outdated style was much more used in the Victorian era. At the later time, I was concerned with their production, and there was a very marked drop in the sale of D.K's.

One can imagine the reluctance of the young female pupils for being "on show", but Miss X. walked amongst them, demonstrating an example of not asking people to do that which she was not prepared to do herself. I think the general babble raised among the remainder of the pupils and, no doubt, the disquiet of the other female staff, that this must have been relayed to the headmaster, and once again, I can only assume that Miss X. was instructed by him, to never cause a similar distraction. As far as I am aware, it never happened again!

Miss X. was certainly a feisty lady!

Narrative 14

IN THE BEGINNING

Among my ventures into the writing of many of my thoughts and memories, I think this article is quite different from all the others. Most of my jottings have been of a light-hearted, sometimes trivial nature, whereas this treatise is of profound character. As the title suggests, it concerns people's attitudes to the question of religion.

To quote the remainder of the title – "In the beginning, God created the universe" (also mankind, creatures and plants); some people accept God as the creator and is recognised as such according to the teaching of Christians (Jesus Christ) and Muslims (Mohammed), even though the attitudes of each differs. God is known by different names by various religious groups – Allah, Baal, Jehovah, Yahweh, Abba, (to name a few).

Some people in the world refuse to accept God, the Creator, and are known as <u>atheists</u>. Some others will not accept God unless it can be proven to them that there is such a power – these are known as <u>agnostics</u>. There is almost no doubt that human beings throughout the world have the <u>inherent desire</u> to believe in an all-powerful influence, because, even the uneducated races from earlier days produced their own idea of authority by selecting, and worshipping their own gods, such as gods of war, thunder, lightning, sun stars, and many other items in nature, - precious gems, various plants and animals etc, and many hand made idols. A lot of people find it difficult to conceive the potency of what our planet earth offers for the existence of mankind, plants and creatures, and when thinking of the universe, is quite beyond the conception of human beings. Astronomers and scientists have studied the stars and planets for hundreds of years, but there are still massive areas to be explored.

To illustrate the size of the problem, I offer the following example to portray the vastness of space, which is the universe. If people were asked if they know the circumference of our <u>own</u>

planet earth, (which is part of the Milky Way galaxy), many would be able to give a good answer but, (in my opinion), I believe that the majority would not answer correctly. The answer is approximately 25,000 miles. Any of our present-day spacecraft travels at a speed of approximately 17,000 miles per hour, so to complete one orbit round the earth takes very approximately one and a quarter hours. Now let us look at distances in space. Time is measured in light years. Light travels at a speed of approximately 186,000 miles per second. This means that if some powerful light was switched on a star, one light year away (at this present moment), it would take one year for it to be seen on our earth, hence the description light year. Most stars and planets are not as close as that, - they extend well out into space to thousands or more light years distance. This means that, if one of our spacecraft could travel at the speed of light, (very, very, approximately 6 million million miles per hour) at present appears an impossibility. Just one more statistic, - the most distant star in our own Milky Way galaxy is about 75 light years distance. Does your mind "boggle" at these figures?

The point I wish to make is to ask, which of us among the human population could say with any degree of certainty that there is no power in the universe, greater than human beings? – we are very little "minnows".

All the statistics already given, only refers to the special environment. What about living things within it? Think about human beings, creatures and plant life. The balance of all this life is phenomenal and astounding. Human beings – if mechanisms in each body are studied, one can only marvel at its systems. The digestive system links through efficient organs to extract the parts of the food the body needs; the blood circulation (via the heart), distributes oxygen to all parts of the body. That oxygen is extracted by our ability to breathe in a mixture of gases like nitrogen, oxygen, carbon dioxide and water, also over ten other gases of minimal quantities, and human lungs extracts that which the body needs most, e.g. oxygen and this is distributed by blood all around the body by a complicated network of tubes (the arteries) to ensure this. A similar network of other tubes (the veins) returns this unclean blood – (it extracts any foreign matter as it proceeds) to the heart which pumps it to the cleaning organs (the lungs) to be reoxygenated for further use. Another set of tubes carries lymph fluid, which retrieves any harmful substances from the blood vessels; this unwanted component, together with fluid and solid waste is cleared from the body. The stomach organ, - liver, secretes bile which aids digestion, particularly fatty food, and two smaller glandular organs, the kidneys, remove more waste from the blood and passes it through the bladder, another important part of the body.

I have only mentioned a number of major organs, but there are very many more, all working in conjunction. Then of course, the brain, - a mini-computer in itself, controls functions of the mind and memory, interconnects actions of the eyes and ears (to give balance), also the sensation of pain if the body gets into trouble. An expert in biology could wax lyrical about the total body's performance. All which has been mentioned has excluded the outward appearance of skin, hair and eyes – all important to an individual. Even this does not account for the body's senses, and the ability to communicate.

Another wonder is the reproduction system and the birth and the eventual death of a person.

Now a brief look at plant life. "Mighty oaks from little acorns grow"– a marvel in itself, but some seeds are so small that they are barely visible, but they bring forth a wonderful array of plants and colours. Plants, too, have a reproductive system, via pollination of a plant's pistil (its seed producing part). All plant life has its life span – some last only for a day and others for many hundred years.

Plants and trees provide shelter and some food for all manner of creatures. Rivers, lakes and oceans for water creatures. The diversity of these are many varieties of mammals, quadrupeds, birds, reptiles, fish, worms, insects and molluscs. The insect population – some single cell, some aquatic, and there is said to be something in the order of 30,000 species. Many live below the surface of the soil (some wizard in figures has estimated that in an average field of cattle, there is as much or more of life weight, engendered by the subsoil life, as the weight of the cattle on the land above them). Some of these small creatures creep on legs, some wriggle along, some have wings and can fly, some can be a nuisance, or even deadly. So, what is their purpose? If we think of the "Web of life" and its working, the minute insects provide the food as they eaten by slightly larger predators, who again, provide the food for the slightly larger ones, which include larger animals and, according to climate and environmental conditions, we see lions, tigers (and all other "cat" varieties, also crocodiles, bears, horses, donkeys, elephants, kangaroos and all manner of dogs (many kept as pets), many varieties of snakes and a multifarious quantity of small creatures mice, rats, moles, voles, squirrels, (in our climate) and hundreds of other varieties in the different climates of the world.

Marine, lake and river life has a multiplicity of water creatures. Some are microscopic and feed on the algae (which are minute, stem-less water plants), and in the same sequence as land creatures, each provide food for the larger ones. These are found in both fresh and salt water. Throughout the world, there are countless hundreds of varieties from the single cell ones, shell fish (food for the wading birds) eels, a magnitude of sizes of fish, in both fresh and salt water, - seals, penguins, sharks, whales, tropical stingrays, and others I cannot immediately name, also.

Of the bird life, I will not attempt to name them – they are too numerous to mention. Bird protection societies and the many bird sanctuaries will convince the reader of the huge varieties.

No doubt you have read this homily so far, and will, by now, be "bored to tears" with statistics, but I wished to write about them (very sketchily) before I summed up the purpose of it.

To begin my concluding thoughts:-

Every activity in the world is motivated by some kind of energy – examples – rubbish scattered in the environment did not appear "by chance", - it needed some power or energy to have thrown it there (thoughtless humans); a fallen apple from a tree - by gravity (another kind of power); an arrow reaching a target (the bow and human effort); money – does not "grow on trees" and does not appear by chance (except by gambling), - coins and notes have needed a lot of energy to produce them, - metal – mining, design, production by the Royal Mint, and many many other examples. Even in space there is still much activity – a report in October 2006 announced the clash of the two galaxies (some 68 light years away), giving birth to countless new stars (Report from the Hubble telescope which is orbiting the earth). All of these activities (except the galaxy clash) emanate from man-made energy. So, what impelling force gives rise to activities in the universe?

Can the human brain comprehend the significance? Would any erudite human suggest that the Creation of the Universe came about by chance? Within the Universe would anyone suggest that the human brain is supreme? (It is pretty good, but!!)?

My own brain allows me to believe that there is some kind of supreme power. Those of us who have a Christian belief, find assurance in naming this, Almighty Power, and are deeply assured when we believe and have faith in a Father Figure. From our early childhood, we have accepted that this Father is everywhere, and watches over our lives. I wonder if atheists can say that no kind of power exists? I don't suppose it will alter their minds, but it could give them "food for thought".

Narrative 15

BITS AND PIECES

Both in my book "Memoirs and Reflections", and my subsequent essays, I have covered quite a range of thoughts. One or two small incidents have "slipped through the cracks!" and in this article, I have filled in with a few memories which come into my thoughts from time to time. All of them are of little consequence, but I still find myself being in a petty state of amused reverie as I occasionally recall them. They are not in chronological order.

1. Let me in!

Films have always been categorised, and in my day, these were "U" films suitable for all ages; "A" films suitable for adults, and "X" films of a horrific nature. At about the age of 15 (last year at school), I decided that I would like to see a particular film (can't remember the title), but I did not realise, until I was about to enter the Pavilion Cinema, that it was an "A" category one. I did not know until the commissionaire said "You can't go in". I was surprised, but the man spoke from the side of his mouth (without looking down at me), "Take your (school) cap off, and put it in your pocket, and then come back". I did as I was told and walked past him as a "grown up". Incidentally, films, mostly being made in Hollywood, were subjected to a kind of censorship under what was called the Hayes Code, with such restrictions as no man and woman could appear together in bed, even if they were portraying a married couple; no nudity; even partially clothed actors must have the bulk of their bodies covered, - standards have certainly changed!

2. Let me out!

Another couple of thoughts about the Pavilion – firstly, the films were projected onto the screen from a projection room at the opposite end of the auditorium, and in the rays of light which traversed the hall, it showed up the massive cloud of cigarette smoke, and the proprietors endeavoured to negate the effect by an attendant, between films, walking up and down the gangways with a pump spray, a handmade pump with a small (soup tin) sized can that contained a pungent scented smell, which pervaded the hall.

The other ditty I will now explain is that, when I was about the age of 7, I went to the matinee performance of a film, popular at the time (probably Harold Lloyd), and the auditorium was filled almost to capacity, I was guided to my seat in the stalls, and it was the front, and on the extreme left. As the screen was little more than 10 feet from the front row, all I could see from my position, (imagine it!), was a thin streak of flickering light! No possible chance of recognising anything on the screen. I left with a violent headache and a twisted neck, and no idea of what the film was about – I felt like shouting "Let me out".

3. Messy days!

Most of us who are native to Kettering, will know that it is referred to as a "Market" town. In fact, in its very early days (pre the Norman Conquest in 1066 AD), it was only a small settlement, and part of a manorial system, under the control of the Abbot of Peterborough. Our Manor House is now used for different purposes. The settlement was probably called Kyteringer, and after 1066, acquired the name of Cytringan.

In the reign of King Henry VII (1216-1272), Kettering, (as its name finally ended up), was granted a Charter, which allowed it to hold a weekly market; there is still very much evidence of those old days – the Market Place, the Horsemarket, the Corn Exchange, the Corn Market Hall, the Cattle Market. It is about this latter market that I wish to make a few comments.

The cattle market (of course now defunct) was held each Friday, and in the early days, farmers drove their cattle herds by road (without vehicles) from outlying villages and farms, into the market stalls, via Kettering's main roads. The railway eased the situation to some extent in the latter part of the 19th Century. Some animals came by goods rail (special trucks), and were then guided by herdsmen through the streets to the stalls. This was an attraction to many folk each Friday – much evidence of retired grandpa's taking their excited grandchildren to see this public display, as they got <u>safely</u> close to the animals and the farming fraternity. All this gave the title of this account as being "messy" which, of course, was inevitable. The cattle droppings of the many cows, also sheep, left the streets in a very dirty state, and its clearance was mainly left to nature to clean it, either by heavy rains, or, after drying out, by the routine street cleaning.

4. Oh, happy day!

Another occasion which was appreciated by children was the Sunday School outing. In earlier days (before my boyhood), children were taken somewhere into the country by horse-drawn wagons, and with the coming of motor vehicles, charabancs or coaches were used. On the particular trip which I remember, getting to our country area was by <u>rail</u>! (even though the location was somewhere in the area of Geddington). We were all given individual child's tickets, and we, in an adult kind of way, had our tickets "clipped" as we passed through the ticket barriers, and then make sure we did not lose the ticket for the return journey. Geddington did not have its own station, but it went to a nearby small village – probably Newton. Britain, at one time had <u>123</u> separate railway companies, covering a mass network of uneconomic lines – many were closed by Dr. Beeching under the pressure of the Government. The small one platform station took us to within a few hundred yards of our field of entertainment. Apart from games played and tea and buns, there was also excitement when sweets were thrown onto the grass and scrambled for. All good fun, but care had to be taken because the field had held cattle, and this, (as with my previous article), it could be a messy operation (most sweets were unwrapped in those days!)

5. Here's health!

Diseases of all sorts have always been with us, although modern medicines are keeping up a reasonable pace with cures and preventive prescriptions. In the early 1930's, illnesses like small pox, tuberculosis, whooping cough and diphtheria were very prevalent, but due to the progression of medicines, the diseases mentioned have all-but died out. Why? One of the discoveries was by an injection of a suitable antidote. Unfortunately, parents at the time, were none to keen to allow their children to be injected, and even today, some parents object to the M.M.R. jab (Measles, Mumps and Rubella), and sometimes with dire consequences.

I want to briefly write about diphtheria. In the 1930's the government tried to persuade parents to have their child injected against it. Many prominent hoardings throughout the land declared "DIPTHERIA IS DEADLY!" – get your child immunised (new description), and I well remember being told by one of my aunties who was friendly with the wife of the hospital's Warden. She said that she had seen mothers who were visiting their own child – one looking hopefully, for any signs of progress detected. Another mother, looking dejectedly at her child in fear and trepidation. Unfortunately, the mother of the second child (who had not been immunised) would, almost certainly not survive! – Sad, but true!

6. Can you hear me?

In the early days of the 20th Century, engineers in a number of countries were experimenting with the possibility of making Sound travel through space, it having been discovered that, under the right conditions, use could be made of air-waves. It needed a piece of equipment to "pick up" sounds, and another, at some distance away, to receive it, and turn it back into the same sound. It seemed like a pipe-dream, but enthusiasts persevered with use of a small piece of crystal, (a colourless transparent mineral), and a fine copper wire (the cat's whisker) plus the use of moving coils (of wire) a valve, many switches and many connecting wires, also the use of both high tension and low tension batteries (the accumulator), and much experimentation, it was possible to "pick up" sound, which could fuzzily, be heard with the use of headphones.

All this excitement encouraged many amateurs to perform this apparent miracle. My brother, Bob, (years older than me), and a friend about 10 houses away along our street, set themselves the task of making some ramshackle equipment, - I think they made the sound receiving box (the microphone) with something like an empty polish tin, and I assume that their receiving device was equally inferior. They asked me to "sing loud" (into the tin!), whilst they went 10 houses up the street to receive it. I must have looked a bit silly singing to a tin, but I gamely complied.

I never got much of an answer from my brother if it had been successful, but I could tell by the look on his face that I had not succeeded as a new "up and coming" artiste!

7. On the ball!

In the present day's of young people's expectations that their leisure time has to be provided for them, in the form of Youth Clubs, etc, my generation had no such back-up except by various Church organisations (Bible Classes, Sunday Schools etc), providing some input, although that was subjected to the rule that they must attend Sunday School, - this restricted a few of them.

Some local councils provided a few playing fields for football, cricket, netball, etc, but not sufficient to accommodate all those who wished to get involved in such games. The real enthusiasts made their own arrangements, by obtaining permission from any farmer, who might have a field suitable for use, and such was the fervour of some small groups, that a few of them took it upon themselves to prepare their own activities. On a Saturday morning, they would purchase a few bags of sawdust for a few pence from a local timber merchant, then cycle with the bag over the handlebars to the farmer's field, - pace out (or use a long roller tape) the pitch area and identified it by a thin line of sawdust, also the other areas – goal area, penalty area, centre line and circle with more sawdust. If they were lucky enough to have goal posts, they would also be set up (no nets!). When all this was prepared, they would return home for their mid-day snack, and then, in their football kit, (shirts, shorts, socks and football boots, would cycle back, play the football game with another team (hail, rain or shine!) and after the game, often covered with mud, would dismantle and store the goalposts, then home for a good wash down – baths, if they were lucky enough – and feel full of satisfaction of the game – (particularly if they won!). That is determination in large measure in the 1930's!

8. On with the shows.

I have never hankered after going "on the stage", but there have been odd times when I have been drawn into such occasions. One of these was when our Central School Scouts and Guides were urged to take part in the production of "Alice in Wonderland" and the sister play "Alice, Through the Looking Glass". Mine were only "bit" parts, but we had good fun rehearsing, and the two plays were presented one after another as one evening's viewing. In the first play I took the small part of the Dodo, organising the ridiculous race, which is how the author Lewis Carroll (pseudonym of Charles Luttwidge Dodson) wrote these two stories (examples – Mad Hatter's Tea Party, Jabberwocky (nonsense) song, etc). I took the small part of the Red King in "Through the Looking Glass".

I was pleased to have also taken part in a production, of Andrew Lloyd Webber's "Joseph and the Technicolour Dreamcoat" which was staged in 2001 by members of Kettering Rockingham Road Baptist Church and friends. Mine was, once again, a small part – Jacob. All these occasions were very good fun!

9. An Impressive Memory.

After my call-up for service in the 1939-45 Second World War, and early promotion to Corporal, part of the preparation for this brought me into very brief contact with a professional Commissioned Officer – Major Pym. I was only in his presence for barely an hour as he conducted a field exercise which required the use of a Camouflage and natural cover (hills, banks, bushes, long grass, etc), to start from a hidden area, and by using the bushes, grass, etc, to move to a position where I could get within about 20 yards of "the enemy" – (Major Pym) and to fire a blank round from my rifle to complete the exercise. I was able to achieve this (with guidance from an instructor), and on completion, I came face to face with the Major for no more than a minute or two. He asked "Have you ever done any kind of field work?" I could only quickly think of a suitable reply and replied "I was a member of a Scout Troop which occasionally explored aspects of the countryside". That ended my brief contact with him.

A couple of years later, I became a Commissioned Officer (Second Lieutenant), and I met up with Major (now Colonel Pym). He briefly looked at my face and amazed me by asking "Were you the Marine who told me you were Boy Scout?" As he came into contact with hundreds of Marines every day, I certainly commend him for a <u>very impressive memory!</u>

10. Cool feet.

In all my life, I can only remember one occasion when the Wicksteed Park Lake was frozen sufficiently solidly for it to bear the weight of skaters – such a year was 1927. It may have iced over on other occasions, but not sufficiently thick and hard for skating. Also, of course, with the emphasis on health and safety, it would, no doubt be forbidden. However on the year in question, (I am fairly sure that was the year), I was 8 years old and my brother Bob, was just over 15 years of age. He took me, with skates for us both, to experience the natural "ice rink". I was very apprehensive, and did not venture far, also my "skating" was extremely "<u>amateurish</u>", but several dozen of local enthusiasts risked it for a day or so. No ice breaking was reported during those exhilarating days, but in certain areas, near the edge of the lake, I became a little jittery, when I heard a <u>creaking</u> sound. I quickly got back to the solid bank. I think I could well have been described as "<u>having cold feet!</u>"

Narrative 16

HISTORY IS BUNK!

Who coined such a phrase, as shown in the title? I am fairly sure that it was credited to the well-known U.S.A. entrepreneur – Henry Ford, the pioneer of the mass-produced motorcar. It is possible it could have been attributed to another person, such as Samuel Goldwyn (of Metro Goldwyn Meyer Film Corporation) but it was certainly a well-respected U.S.A. industrialist in the early 20th Century.

I used this expression because I want to write about the importance of history, also other subjects, which are taught in our schools. We often hear complaints about what is the importance of the study of the range of subjects being taught? Such grumbles often come from leaders of industry, who suggest that more practical subjects would be better. I give my reasoning of what is gained by learning about almost the full range of those taught up to secondary school levels.

HISTORY

For some people, history lessons may not be entertaining as a study, but the content is <u>constantly growing</u>. News of <u>any</u> kind today, becomes <u>recent</u> history after a short time and <u>ancient</u> history over the course of centuries. With this thought in mind, I let my mind cogitate into the <u>purpose</u> of it being taught (history and most other subjects studied in schools) some people say that present teaching methods do not produce educated brains. So, let me look at each subject and explain what I think is their importance. We may, or may not, have given thought about <u>our own</u> recent <u>family</u> background, but a lot of people have become interested in their ancestors (sometimes with a few surprises!) – certainly an interesting history!

History covers not only our own country's past records, but the world (in terms of how one country relates to others). Many of the world's conflicts are engendered because of bad relationships with neighbouring countries. One example is the result of the ending of the First World War 1914-18, when Germany was dispossessed of certain countries under its control (Treaty of Versailles) and with rise to power of Adolf Hitler, from 1933, he claimed that Germany needed more "living space" and his armies marched into some of these areas, without permission or a fight, to regain them for Germany. The apparent ease with which he regained these states led him to venture into other countries – Austria, Czechoslovakia, and finally Poland, which woke up <u>our</u> country to attempt to put a stop to this, thus the Second World War, - certainly history!

In 1215 A.D. King John was persuaded to sign the Magna Carta, which established people's personal and political liberty, which holds <u>good today</u>. This also helped to develop the Common Law. This is <u>unwritten,</u> but many Courts of Law decisions are based on the laws from many years ago, and the judgement of today's special cases sometimes added to the existing ones and become a "bench-mark" for the judgement of similar cases.

I would think that most people will have heard of King Henry VIII (1509-1547). He created much religious controversy; the fact that he was unable to father a son (for succession), and the inability of most of his six wives to conceive one. (The life of his various wives ended in tragedy, - one died, and one, Anne Boleyn, was beheaded. Henry himself died at the age of 38 with a sexual disease!), brought him to a stage of such petulance that he took drastic action. Apart from two daughters, Mary (Mary Queen of Scots) and Elizabeth (Elizabeth I who succeeded Henry) he demanded a divorce from one of his last wives, and this was <u>denied by the Pope</u> at that time. This so frustrated Henry that he <u>abolished</u> the Roman Catholic Church in this country, and established the Church of England (The Reformation). Incidentally, Henry had a <u>second wife</u> (Katherine Howard – beheaded!)

History is so full of important information, but I will only quote one other incident about Oliver Cromwell. He was the leader of the Puritans that fought a war against the Monarchy. (The English Civil War), and Cromwell ordered the execution of King Charles I, and he <u>banished</u> the Monarchy, and for about a decade, England was a <u>Republic!</u> One final word, - because of the feuding between the Roman Catholic and the Church of England, clandestine members of the R.C. Church, (Guy Fawkes and others), planned to "blow up" Parliament! It is now remembered as Bonfire Night. Read up many more fascinating historical stories.

GEOGRAPHY

Britain is a trading nation – there is insufficient land to grow food for all the population – so it is important that we keep trading with most other countries of the world.

During the days of our naval explorers, (James Cook, Christopher Columbus, Francis Drake and others), they set out to discover new lands, and when established, became part of the British Empire (now the British Commonwealth).

When I was in primary education, (5-7 years of age), our teacher had spoken of the importance of Great Britain in the world, and she displayed a large world map over the blackboard, and a huge area was <u>coloured red,</u> - all the countries of the <u>Empire</u>. She asked if anyone in the class could point out Great Britain on the map, and it was then shown to us with a pointer. I was almost overcome with surprise when she indicated the <u>very tiny</u> British Isles, and the country responsible for the growth of such a large Empire.

Development of some of the poorer countries has grown over the centuries, and these have become important trading nations, and whilst in the early days of Empire growth, Britain was given privileged trade preference, which made our imports and materials very adequate, but now we need to ensure that our exports to countries with whom we must trade, are of <u>top quality value,</u> in order that we can buy adequate goods from them in return.

British citizens today seek to holiday in some of the exotic countries of the world which have been vastly updated to make them attractive to tourists. Geography also teaches us of danger areas of the world, - possibly of earthquakes, tsunami, hurricanes, etc. Britain, to date, has been a temperate area, and less prone to such upheavals.

ENGLISH

Our "Mother-tongue" developed over many hundreds of years, with languages brought to us by many invaders – Romans, Normans,

Vikings, Norsemen, Jutes and others. Parts of their languages were absorbed into the language of the Angles, Saxons and the other various words used by the Picts, Scots, Welsh and Irish inhabitants and this has brought about the richest language in the world. There are so many ways of expressing the same subject. A standard English dictionary has over 100,000 words and definitions, and whilst a learned scholar would find it practically impossible to know, and explain the meaning of them all, the choice is wide and interesting.

No-one would debar the introduction of new words also the influence of the U.S.A. (their usage of our English language) also words from the many day-to-day vocabulary which are introduced by books, newspaper and the radio and television, also our regular conversations. (New dictionary editions are regularly brought out to include these words). Some jargon is included which is brought about by text messages. People using little else but text language, will find it difficult to understand the full "range of English".

We should differentiate between the different kinds of English – conversational, business, technical, standard, poetic and of course, the slip shod use of slang!

A child will get a better start in understanding the language if parents show their youngsters how book reading can be fun, starting with the simplest ones, and moving onto more difficult ones by easy stages. Sadly, there are some parents who, themselves, were not encouraged to read and appreciate books as they grew up. Schools cannot be responsible for making up for the early lack of interest.

English is used in many countries to supplement their own language, but surely, we Britons ought to have a good command of our own native tongue!

MATHEMATICS

Before the introduction of calculators, adding machines and the like, infant and junior school children had to go through regular repetitive "grind" of learning the times-tables, by rote. In retrospect, I was glad this was so, when you occasionally find someone who struggles with figures like 9 x 7, or 7 x 8, or even simpler ones like 3 x 8. Also the necessary monotonous practice of adding columns of figures, also subtractions and divisions. In junior school, these were regularly tested mentally, but it became "second nature" to each of us.

When I think about the use of algebra or trigonometry in adult life, we cannot see the significance of their use, that is probably true for most of us, but it certainly gets the brain working!

Exercises in money values are vital, but nowadays is less complicated than in the days of pounds, shillings and pence (£.s.d) currency. The use of averages and percentages does get regular use in life, and it is as well that we should be able to understand and calculate them.

SCIENCE AND PHYSICS

A pupil will almost certainly be better prepared to tackle these two subjects if he, or she, has a good knowledge and practise of Mathematics, because of the use of many formulae used to calculate the results of experiments. At the present time (2000A.D.), concern has been raised about the possible shortage of scientists and physicists in the country. It has some most excellent exponents of each, but there is evidence that some British students steer clear of them as being too laborious. I would say that those succeeding in the subjects could have a lucrative future!

LANGUAGES

The choice of a foreign language to be taught is arbitrary, and a school will choose one which seems to be appropriate. Common choices are French, German and Spanish, which have a fairly wide usage in the world, but for anyone wishing to specialise in a subject, would need a further course of study. What is taught in schools is usually adequate enough to enable one say to be understood on a holiday visit to the country.

Quite a number of large sized firms these days employ someone with language skills to interpret transactions for the export trade.

PHYSICAL EDUCATION AND GAMES

Schools are required to make provision for these subjects for the obvious benefit it gives to the health of young pupils.

OTHER SUBJECTS

Some schools choose to specialise in some particular sphere of study, of other subjects, but generally encourage the use of computer technology which is now quite much used within the population.

Drama and Art are usually included in the basic syllabus which makes a break from concentrated studies and may encourage the appreciation of "the arts" in later life. Domestic science and needlework are very often included for the girls, (boys ought to know how to boil an egg!!) In the case of my school days (early 1930's), handicrafts, woodwork, metalwork etc, were included for the boys, also some technical drawings.

TO CONCLUDE

There seems these days that an attitude has developed suggesting that any of these subjects taught will be of no practical use in later life. I hope that, by my brief descriptions, some of the information may not be of a practical nature, but is more of an important background for all that goes on daily, but it should be understood that some subjects, like algebra, geometry and mental testing are not taught just for the content but to exercise the brain to the extent that, whatever problems arise, a person is capable of thinking through for a solution – quite vital!

The final point I want to make is that many employers today, seem to believe that those leaving school should be capable of fitting in as an employee for their own line of business, but the variety of these is very wide ranging; there is no way, that an employer should expect that a school leaver's ability will suit every kind of work. What the employer should expect is that a potential employee should have the ability to read and write, thus comprehend instructions given to them (sadly some fail to achieve this), but it should be the employer's responsibility to train the new employee to the standards he/she requires for his/her business needs in the workplace.

Schooling needs concentration but, today, many pupils approach it too casually. (Good instructors, special cases, day release etc).

These are all vital for success!

Narrative 17

PET'S CORNER

I am writing about pets, not as an owner but one who appreciates their importance in the right circumstances.

When I was young, I pleaded with my mother to allow me to have a pet rabbit – I promised that I would look after it, feed it, exercise it as the occasion arose, also to keep the cage clean. Did I keep my promise? – No! I appreciated that I had got a pet, but my mother was put into the invidious position of doing most of the things I promised to do. My pet met a sad end, - whilst I was allowing it to exercise itself on our reasonably sizeable lawn (fenced round), I did not bargain for the small terrier dog of the neighbour next door – suddenly it gave a loud bark and ran down to the lawn fencing (with me breathlessly chasing it!). It found a gap, large enough for it to be able squeeze through, and it pounced onto the rabbit's neck, and it immediately lay dead – to my horror.

I think that as a result of my loss, I looked at pet keeping from a slightly different standpoint. When my own two children were becoming interested in the possibility of owning a pet, my line of reply was, that if they owned one, they must do all the necessary things, as I indicated above, and that if the pet was a dog, the exercise part meant <u>them</u> taking it "walkies". If at the end of a particularly hectic, or worrying day's work, I would not allow myself to become routined by a regular plea at bedtime – "Dad, - the dog needs a walk". I did not wish to be drawn into such a regularity.

We did have one or two pets which did not need such exercise – a number of budgerigars, but I was not keen on having them fluttering around in a confined space to give them a break from being caged, also the difficulty of persuading them back into the cage afterwards. We also had a guinea pig which squawked incessantly when anyone was close to the cage.

I wasn't completely heartless, because my sister Pauline had a pet dog and, as she was working for a few hours daily, my wife Barbara, offered to look after it for the few hours she was at work. I took it upon myself to prepare its daily meal, by chopping up all the food; it was now getting to the age when its teeth were getting incapable of chewing the food.

There is a huge variety of pets which people keep, and I agree that in a lot of circumstances a pet is good – the lonely people, those who are housebound, those keen on exercising with a pet, a real pet lover, and so on, but whatever the circumstances, pets <u>need care</u>. It seems to me to be most unwise for a puppy to be gifted to a young child however excited they appear to be. The pet will grow and <u>need attention</u> which they sometimes do not get. Some, irresponsibly, turn them out onto the street to become unwanted strays! Cats need to be let out daily, and they will wander for long distances, they will return, but, if they meet up with the male of the species – (let's call him Tom), it will not be long before there is a litter of them. Will the pet owner be prepared to look after them? Have you enough willing friends to receive a pet? – it must be considered, unless a "vet" has been paid to neuter your pet.

If a young cat wanders too far from home to return safely, it is possible that it may become a little "wild" in its activities and, if it joins with a group of other wild ones, it becomes feral, and remains in a wild state with its new found group.

Probably the people's favourite is the dog species – too numerous to name them all, but very many are well known breeds, often thoroughbreds which, by constant in-breeding, can sometimes be highly-strung in their early life, but calm down as they grow. A mongrel can be a very loyal pet, depending on the breeds of their parents.

Some choose the well- known kind of house dogs, but others think in "exotic" terms, and choose such creatures as deadly spiders, and I have known about a couple of young men who kept rats in cages, - <u>in their bedroom!</u> Most unhygienic I would think! Other strange choices are snakes, alligators, even small tigers (which become too large to handle). No doubt the tiger was purchased in its kitten state. There was a local case a few years ago (probably around 2003/4) when a person had two small ostriches, which were kept in a relatively small back garden. No doubt great fun to see them scamper round as young birds, but he (and his neighbours) became worried as they grew into adult birds. The last I saw of them was when the heads and a good deal of their long necks were visible over the five foot brick garden wall. I do not know what became of them, but at that stage, they suddenly disappeared.

The greatest number of pets kept by the average British family is the dog species; they also feature in sporting and farming circles. Farmers find them invaluable when moving flocks of sheep. In the sporting world, the breed used is hounds for fox hunting (still undertaken in spite of curbing parliamentary regulation). Whippets and greyhounds are used in racing; suitable dogs trained to guide blind people, and bloodhounds for police work. There is such a wide variety of domestic pets that I won't attempt at naming them all. However, I do wish to make one or two comments about a few species. In the light of recent reports (Oct. 2006) of the Rottweiler dogs <u>killing</u> a baby, and a second case within a day or so of that incident, another young child was <u>savaged</u> by a Rottweiler, I am convinced, in my own mind, that whilst that breed may well be good to guard property, they are too large as domestic pets, similarly such breeds as Bull Terriers, Bulldogs and other kinds which are required, by law, to be muzzled when mixing with people, - they may be "loved" by their owners (or possibly kept as a kind of status symbol!), but they do not seem to be a good breed as house pets. But, everyone has their own tastes.

Whatever pet is acquired as a puppy, it pays dividends training them to reasonable commands. It can be frustrating with a young and excitable pup, but if they are left to get their own way, without suitable control, the owner may regret it later. Other treasured pets are horses, for those who wish to ride. They need a good stable and meadow space for regular exercise and daily checks, so it requires <u>dedication</u>. Another pet is the tortoise – they need a reasonable space to move around, and a place for their hibernation. In a garden, they have been known to burrow under a fence into a neighbour's garden.

The last thing I would say about pets, - they need the services of a vet, and they can be <u>very expensive</u>.

Good luck to those who own a pet.

Narrative 18

BRITISH CITIZENSHIP

The name <u>British Constitution</u> describes the way a country organises its way of life, behaviour and character of its people. British life is very much influenced by many aspects which we experience. Native British born members receive guidance on everyday occurrences by their parents who, if they are true to the commonly accepted style of "Britishness", will introduce some thoughts from a very early age, principally by their own actions.

More examples are illustrated by other citizens, with whom they come into contact in their daily lives – friends, neighbours, relatives, etc. and later when starting to school. Incidentally, schools do not teach it as a subject, but their importance is brought to bear by children being together experiencing the best way to relate to many others with a variety of moods and disposition.

Immigrant citizens, some of whom will be completely unfamiliar with any, or all of these guardian influences, and often with no ability, other than a smattering of the English language would be almost at a complete loss to comprehend the alien, to them, way of life, as we would find if we went, completely unprepared, into their countries. There have been suggestions, particularly in the early decades of the 21st century, that these new citizens should undergo a course in the English Language so that they can more clearly understand our way of life.

Apart from the regular subjects studied in infant, junior and secondary schools, such as reading, writing, arithmetic, history, geography, artistic sessions, etc., there is no formal lesson on the constitution. Personally, I feel that this subject is extremely important; I have, in this article, set out the subjects I consider important influences on our lives in fact, during my 21 years teaching time on general education in technical colleges, I introduced them whenever I could use them, within the syllabus laid down.

In this article, I have set out the subjects, which I believe are relevant to both British born, and immigrant youngsters and elders, which have an important influence on our manner of living, namely the British Constitution. The subjects listed are not set out in any order of importance.

LAW AND ORDER

a) Common law (unwritten) and case law
b) Courts of law – Criminal, Civil, County Courts. Petty sessions.
c) Judges, juries, Barristers, Solicitors.
d) Legal Aid.

PARLIAMENT

a) Elections – Parliamentary parties, Prime Minister, Ministers, and Members of Parliament.
b) Importance of voting (elections can be lost/won by few votes.)
c) Types of elections – first past the post, proportional representation by transferable votes (coalition), discussion re strong government and coalitions mention difficulties of Italian coalitions post 2nd World War.
d) The Civil Service
e) Stages of Law Making – Green Paper, 1st, 2nd Reading Committee Stage, 3rd Reading confirmed by Monarch's signature.

LOCAL ELECTIONS

a) County Councils}
b) Local Councils }   and various services, listed later.
c) Parish Councils }
   EDUCATION
a) Primary – (Infant and Junior)

b) Secondary
c) Tertiary
d) Technical Colleges
e) Special Schools (e.g. handicapped)
f) Higher Education (Various Universities)
g) Examinations/Degrees etc.

RELIGIONS OF THE WORLD

a) Roman Catholic
b) Church of England (High and low)
c) Islam
d) Hindu
   (Baptist, United Reformed)
e) Sikh
f) Salvation Army
g) Buddha
h) Pentecostal
i) Seventh Day Adventists
j) Jehovah's Witness
k) Christian Brethren
l) Plymouth Brethren
   Orders – Numeries

m) Society of Friends
n) Shinto
o) Taoism
p) Free Churches

q) Methodist
r) Presbyterian
s) Jesus Army
t) Episcopal
u) Mormon
v) Unification
w) Scientology
x) Monastic

(Plus campaigners, House groups, Sects, gods, idols etc.) also atheism and agnosticism.

CRIMINAL ACTIVITIES

a) Street crime
b) Burglary
c) Sentences
d) Probation
e) Summons
f) Charges
g) Bail
h) ASBO's

NEIGHBOURHOOD

Variable – (elite or rowdy) according to owners, tenants, etc. (which make them reasonable or poor)

HOUSING

Private owners, Council stock, Private let out for rental, Housing Associations, (importance of suitable sites, - flooding, subsidence etc.)

Owners responsible for upkeep of the structure

Both owners and tenants responsible for keeping them free of rubbish and general tidiness – dangers of fly tipping

CITIZENS RIGHTS & RESPONSIBILITIES

Rights	Responsibilities
Free Speech	Do not inflame others to cause a fracas.
Freedom to travel	Do not take troubles to other places to disturb peace (example football hooligans)
Freedom of assembly	Do not cause road blocks, - choose suitable venues to minimise troubles (example Glastonbury Festival), also Speakers Corner – Hyde Park.
Freedom to listen to Radio/TV	Do not download pornography or other offensive materials
The Right to vote	Some people do not vote because no candidate is suitable – but VOTE for the least worst candidate (if all took the same views, there would be no government.) N.B. in a dictatorship voting is very limited or banned completely.

CIVIL LIBERTIES

a) A democracy <u>needs rules</u> of behaviour (like a game of sport)
b) Police have the power to stop-search doubtful behaviour.
c) Restriction placed on people sometimes construed as loss of liberties.
d) Landowners do not like complete freedom of countryside.
e) Landowners make money with the use of land for fox hunting, shooting etc.
f) Civil liberties groups speak up for such people, and any others who believe they are being "picked on". N.B. – freedoms in our country are much greater than some countries.

CIVIC PRIDE - pride is defined as satisfaction and pleasure of one's actions.

a) Pride in own home environment already mentioned. This should extend to neighbourhoods, villages, towns and cites.
b) It needs concerted action by <u>all</u> people to achieve this.

GOVERNMENT SERVICES

a) Police (Metropolitan and area forces)
b) Fire Services – important to have adequate cover.
c) Waste clearance (county authorities)
d) Housing (local authorities)
e) Waste recycling (local authorities)
f) Highways and road networks – National Government's Highway Agency with responsibility for keeping reasonable traffic flow, safety, road direction signs, dangerous speed driving, repairs etc.

TAXATION RATES (differentiate!)

a) Taxation raised by government for services provided.
b) Rates levied by Local Authorities to cover cost of services.

HEALTH SERVICES

a) Paid for by charitable donations until the National Health Service commenced in 1948.

b) Covers the whole range of peoples' needs.
c) Accident and Emergency departments at strategic points.
d) Specialist hospitals for a wide range of illnesses e.g. cancer, heart, sexual diseases etc.
e) Maternity units.

GENERAL PRACTITIONERS (G.P'S)

a) Everyone entitled to be treated by a GP (general and dental)
b) Wide range of suitable drugs available
c) Co-operation with hospital facilities (Appointment dates/ times etc.)

CARE HOMES

a) For the elderly who need a little guidance
b) Nursing Homes for those who also need nursing care

HOME HELPS

a) For those needing a little help (wash/dress etc.)
b) Also provision of domestic help for house cleaning
c) Meals on wheels.

MILITARY FORCES

a) Government raised and funded – Army, Navy and Air Force
b) Territorial Army – trained soldiers continuing part-time.
c) Department for ordering all necessary arms and equipment.

MI5 AND MI6

a) Highly trained departments to maintain security both at home and abroad

INDUSTRY AND COMMERCE

a) Mainly privately run industrial companies both large and small dealing with all products needed.

b) Commerce companies deal with the many services needed by industry
c) Companies can be large or small with capital directed by the stock exchange (larger companies) or private capital (smaller companies).
d) Some may be partnerships with workers having a controlling interest, and some co-operative industrial units with worker participation or Co-operative Retail, with members having a hand in control

BANKS, FINANCE HOUSES, BUILDING SOCIETIES

a) Finance houses and Banks provide capital to business
b) Building Societies provide loans for housing
c) Banks and Building Societies (a few <u>mutual</u> control) provide facilities for savings – competitive interest offered
(explain "<u>mutual</u>")

INSURANCE COMPANIES

a) Offer a range of services – true insurance, whole life insurance, endowment insurances (differentiate each)

MONARCHY versus REPUBLIC

a) Britain's present Monarch Queen Elizabeth II has been our Head of State for 52 years (as at 2007) without elections.
b) Inherited wealth (Crown Estates etc.) assigned over to the British taxpayer. In return, the Monarch is allocated a suitable sum to live on.
c) Republics have <u>elected</u> Heads of State. Some countries ruled by doubtful characters, and need periodic re-election (costly!)
d) The British Monarch is a titular Head of State and has no jurisdiction over the making of laws

SOCIAL SERVICES

The range of services provided by the Government via the taxpayer to assist people when needed by financial help for the unemployed, ill, disabled, etc. (refer to the "cheats")

WORK ETHIC

The necessity (for most people) to earn a living, to provide a means of existence. The British moral principle – "if you do not work, you do not eat!"

PLANNING AND NATIONAL PARKS

a) The need to plan areas for living space and industrial needs
b) To control "ribbon development" (e.g. building out from city and town centres along a main road, leaving no depth of development.
c) National Parks are set aside, free from bulk buildings, with free access by the public to enjoy.
d) Also areas of natural beauty
e) Sites of special Scientific Interest (SSSI's)

TRADE UNIONS

a) Their origins, some of their successes and failures
b) Present day needs (for bargaining with one voice with employers)

EUROPEAN MEMBERSHIP

a) It's constitution
b) Consider the choice of Britain joining

SPORTS AND LEISURE FACILITIES

a) Government grants where practicable
b) Many organised by Local Government
c) Some organised by groups or societies

VOLUNTARY ORGANISATIONS

a) Alcoholic & Drug (anonymous groups) etc
b) Many local groups (Scouts, Guides, Boys' Brigade, Army Cadets, Naval Cadets, etc.)
c) Occasional grants, made by authorities to keep young people "off the streets"

TRUSTS AND CHARITIES (very similar, but initially set up differently)

a) Trust set up, (often by benevolent citizens) by the provision of a grant, thereafter controlled by a committee of Trustees to follow the wishes of the original grantee. They often attempt to boost the funds by any means of earnings.

b) Charities – usually set up to fund some kind of need. Reliant on charitable gifts, also they attempt to boost their funds by whatever means, (prize draws, etc.) Run by volunteers, but large groups needing management skills, paid officials.

SUGGESTED METHODS OF APPLICATION

Precursory thoughts – Immigrants will certainly need to have an idea of any country to which they emigrate.

Native born Britain's do not get any formal education on this subject, but mainly concentrate on the three R's, History, Geography, Mathematics, Science, Sports activities, etc. but many, even in later life, do not fully appreciate our way of life.

My own thoughts

I do not believe there can be any meaningful tuition at either the Infant or Junior schooling levels, although during these early years, reference may be made to such services as police, fire services, doctors, hospitals etc. etc.

a) For British- born pupils, my own idea is to commence to talk and teach the elements of the Constitution from the beginning of their Secondary Education.

b) The total list of all the subjects considered to be important to be divided into approximately thirty sessions. These to be accommodated by one teaching period each week from the age of 11 plus – each group of ten taking one school year approximately. This would leave the final (examination) years free for examination purposes. If desired, a weekly period to review what has been taught so far.

c) I would issue every 11 plus pupil with a stiff-covered, clip ring –folder with a title "BRITISH CONSTITUTION" and a short preamble introduction and space set aside on the inside cover for a pupil's name.

d) This folder would be used for the remainder of their school years and whatever weekly information is taught, an A5 sized hand-out is placed into the folder. At the end of their school days, they would possess a fairly brief complete summary of all the information studied.

e) School leavers will have a permanent record of all the studies.

Immigrant studies to follow the same pattern but greatly condensed to provide the record as they relate to society.

Narrative 19

<u>KETTERING'S JEWEL OF LEISURE</u>

I included the description "Jewel" in the title because I am delighted to pay tribute to the benefactor who set up the Wicksteed Park, Kettering. He was Mr Charles Wicksteed who came from Leeds, his home area in Yorkshire, to establish a business in general engineering at the time when Kettering was rapidly developing due to industrial growth at the latter part of the 19th Century. He opened his works in 1871, and he soon became involved in the activities of the general public. In addition to evolving a thriving business, he also had a benevolent nature. He served on both the Kettering Urban (as it was then) District Council and the Northamptonshire County Council.

Because of his fertile imagination, he let his mind visualise some kind of play area for the very young children. He had noticed the great pleasure shown by some young Sunday School children playing on very primitive wooden framed swings, and his "mechanised" mind guided him to the thought that they would be safer and more serviceable if made from metal. He set to work having swings produced at his own workshops, - but, where would they be sited? They needed space, and his agile mind led him to become a local benefactor. He purchased about a 150 acre tract of land between Kettering and Barton Seagrave, and the southern end, contained a small tributary river (the Ise), and the northern end was reasonably flat, and it was in the latter area that Mr Wicksteed had the strong swings erected. This open recreational space became known as the Wicksteed Park, and from that simple start in 1921, he formulated new play equipment. He devised things like see-saws (one child at each end), maypoles, and long seated plank (safety grips between seats), and this was suspended at each end by two metal arms, which were pivoted at the top of a strong metal frame, also pivoted onto the plank. This allowed it to swing horizontally, and gave great pleasure to children (occasionally adult passengers)

– it was sometimes referred to as the "jazz". A similar plank-seated ride was suspended by triangular metal arms, which just had <u>one</u> pivotal point at the top. This allowed the long seating to swing, like a floating see-saw (fairground swing boat style). It could be worked to great heights by an energetic person at each end using their body movement. Of course, we had a few idiotic teenage males who "showed off", by working it to the extent that the platform (no passengers!) reached an almost 180° elliptical swing, and at that point, one of the teenage "power force" would (perilously) jump off when his end reached ground level, while his partner at the other end would give one final burst of its speed and then, also, jump clear – I have seen, very occasionally, the final outcome of this stupid practice, of the long seated plank going right over the top (360°), and dangerously continuing to swing until it came to a stop.

This was brought to the attention of Mr W, who, by his wizardry, devised safety brakes near the top pivot so that it would <u>never</u> let this happen again! Slides of all lengths with <u>shiny</u> brass surfaces, gave excitement to children of all ages. The very young had a safer "take-off" with a box safety cage.

In approximately 1926 (about 5 years after the park opened), Mr Wicksteed often questioned any youngsters who he found playing on any of this new equipment, and it was on one such occasion that I briefly met him (the only time I did) as I was playing with one or two other young ones. "Hello, boys," he said, "are there any more things you would like to see and use in the park?" We could not muster a quick enough thought to make any useful suggestions, but that did not deter him from maintaining his own thoughts on new and novel games. One such unusual amusement was a circular frame and seating, suspended on a strong conical frame, with a strong metal cone cup; a ball bearing which rested on the extremely strong central pole, enable the complete frame and seating to, not only move round in a circular motion, but up and down, to create a rolling wave effect – very good fun for the youngsters (and a few mums and dads!)

Also introduced were a small variety of roundabouts of probably an approximately 10 feet diameter. One was a simple round platform, segmented by safety grip rails, and a similar one with platform raised seating level. There was also a five or six seater rocking horse. Provision also for the more athletic children, - a climbing frame, a ladder fixed horizontally to enable the energetic ones to traverse its length by hand over hand movements along the rungs. For the real sporty type, there was a series suspended ropes with strong rings at the ends, so that those with muscular arms could swing along the line of rings (similar to those professionally provided for athletic displays).

In the early years of the park, a fairly large circular sandpit was provided with a raised central deck onto which the children could build sandcastles. I think over a number of years, it was found that pets also enjoyed the romp in the sand, and it became unhygienic and discontinued. Still thinking about sport, in the early years a number of tennis courts were made available, also a small suitably sized golf course. Nor were pet lovers forgotten, because in the 1930's a small selection of unusual birds of the world were displayed in a wire netted compound, (which gave the birds reasonable exercise space) and a small pet zoo. All the attractions so far mentioned were completely free to use.

In 1926 came another invention – the water-chute, and is still very popular at the present time (2006). In the early 1930's came another new novelty – the miniature railway. It was able to carry almost 100 people on each trip and, at busy times, was hauled by two separate engines – 'King Arthur' and 'Lady of the Lake'. The total length of the track is almost one and a half miles, as it started somewhere near the centre of the park, which Mr Wicksteed planned by damming a small river, (which I mentioned), to fill about three and a half acre lake. At one point, the engine and carriages pass through a long tunnel (probably about 30 yards).

Apart from the lake being a desirable addition to the park, it also brought into being the elements of boating. It was divided into a large area for 4 or 6 seater rowing boats, and a smaller area for kiddie's paddle boats. The lake was considered sizeable enough to hold regattas – I remember one or two in the early years being organised by the rowing club. The expanse of water was also large enough to employ a motor-launch, giving trips for a dozen or so people each trip. Also in the earlier years, a small extension from the side of the lake drew water into a small safe graduated area for children to paddle, under the watchful eye of parents.

There was also an oval track of about 30-40ft dimension, which provided miniature racing cars for children to "race" around the track. Provision was made for the possibility of inclement weather by a sizeable round shelter, fairly close to the children's play area. Also provided was a cinema which could be opened during bad weather. In the 1930's a good sized cycle track was laid, but this did not get used to its full potential.

Of course there was catering available, and a large distinctive building, referred to as the Wicksteed canteen, but this name does not do justice to its importance. It certainly catered for the thousands of day trippers, by serving jugs of tea, sandwiches, a variety of cakes and other confectionery, but within this building is a very large hall suitable for dancing, public meetings and large celebrity occasions, also a series of small suites suitable for business meetings, receptions, family gatherings, etc., and this is supported by excellent chefs and efficient staffing. They cater for many nationally known events. In the 1930's, the Trust (Wicksteed Village Trust, set up by Mr Wicksteed) began to make its own distinctive ice-cream, which has won a number of awards. I spoke of the building as being impressive, and it is made so by the large flat roof having a superimposed box-shaped addition, from which a fairly tall tower is built up from its centre, to display a four faced large clock, which is visible from a good deal of the park. I understand that there is the possibility of some kind of grant being made available for use over the next year or so, (2007 onwards), and the Trustees also wish to apportion part of it for the complete refurbishment of this brasserie area, also more shelter in case of bad weather.

Some people take the view that because Mr Wicksteed's conception of the facilities was to provide free or inexpensive pleasure for people in Kettering, that it is a kind of charity, and that therefore car parking charges for Kettering people should also be free. We should understand that the income from parking charges helps to maintain a good permanent staff for full time duties, both in and out of seasons, also the host of part-time staff during the summer season. It is not a profit making organisation, and any surpluses (depending on weather conditions, etc) are used to provide new amusements, quite a number are those used by commercial entertainment venues.

I did not mention Mr Wicksteed's faithful companion – his dog, Jerry, which accompanied him on most of his travels. Upon the dog's death, his "master" had a small sculpted figure of Jerry, together with a worded inscription placed in the rose garden, laid in conjunction with a bandstand.

As the park was built in the Kettering boundaries, it was certainly appreciated by the townsfolk, but "being on our own doorstep", we did not show the same degree of enthusiasm, as it was always there whenever we wanted to use it. On the other hand, it attracts many hundreds of thousands of visitors during the recognised open season from a very wide area – coaches, special trains, private cars etc, arrive to allow their passengers to enjoy a very special day.

I remember in the year approximately 1927; there was a severe cold winter which caused the lake to freeze quite solidly. Many local skaters took advantage of this situation by using the lake as a rink. I was aged about 8 years old, and my brother Bob, obtained skates for himself and I, to take part. (I did not skate – I "wobbled"!) – it was good fun. That is the only year I remember the lake icing over, but I am informed, that on one or two other winter occasions, the lake was partially drained, which allowed a much safer skating surface. No doubt, modern Health and Safety Regulations would not allow it now.

Due to my age and walking difficulties, also my absence due to the war service years, plus employment in North Lincolnshire, I have not been able to visit the park for many years, but I believe that some of the things I have described have necessitated being re-designed or removed to comply with all the new Health and Safety Regulations. This also, sadly, apparently, caused the cessation of the production of the delicious ice-cream.

So finally I say, Hail, then to the benevolent Mr Charles Wicksteed – deceased 1931. A wonderful and gracious citizen.

Narrative 20

<u>MEGALOMANIA</u>

The title word is to be found in the Oxford English dictionaries. It is defined in two ways – "a form of <u>madness</u>, in which a person has exaggerated ideas of his or her <u>own importance</u>", the second one – "an obsessive desire to do things on a <u>grand scale</u>".

I would like to make some observations about the truth, or otherwise, of the implications raised by the dictionary definitions. Much of the truth lies in the inherent make-up of men and women, - both the present generation, and that of earlier history. What are some of the basic human natures? The following points must have some place in the list, - angriness, greed, hatefulness, jealousy, violence, mischievousness, molestation, prejudice, harassment, persecution, evil thoughts or actions such as manslaughter, murder etc, and all the ramifications that each carry. The opposing descriptions of those are such things as loyalty, love, justice, trustworthiness, having principles, good faith, fairness, honour, truthfulness, respect – (there are others), but many of these are in short measure within the population.

Looking at the first (the "angry") part of those listed, it is not true to say that our ancestors were free of such things, and in fact, they can still be extensively found in some present day countries of the world. The United Kingdom, it appears to me, seems to have more than a fair share of them, also in my view, getting more evident. Likewise, it is my belief that humans with an adequate amount of the qualities in their make up (as shown in the second part of the listing), life for all the people in the world, would be less harsh in general terms. Historical explorations of ancient sites have revealed many horrors of the savage activities in many countries, including our own, and the one in Pompeii, near Naples, Italy, revealed the damage caused by the volcanic eruption of Vesuvius in AD69. In the volcanic ash were found not only the bodies of the people, but pictures still hanging in the ruined houses depicting pornography at that time.

Whilst a large number of countries have disposed of <u>legal</u> execution, (including our own), forms of punishment in earlier times included men, and women, being "put in the stocks"; or worse still suffering the pain of the thumbscrew, cat o'nine tails, burning at the stake, (particularly those described as witches); violent stretching of bodies on the rack; hung (gibbet) drawn and quartered; flogging, particularly of sailors; flogging by birch, (including young offenders); caning, particularly unruly children at school; beheading; death by hanging. Note these were all accepted as <u>legal</u> according to laws in force at the time. Our own death penalty was last used around the mid 1960's when the <u>last woman</u> to be hung was Ruth Ellis, for killing her cheating lover, just prior to the abolition of this penalty. Many people today believe that hanging should be re-introduced. It may appear seemly to them, in order to curb some present day crime, but it would be overwhelmingly opposed. Christians, of course, have written decree within the Ten Commandments – "Thou shalt not commit murder" – that also implies that <u>no other</u> person should be asked to execute another on your behalf.

Many problems arise because of the meandering and unfaithfulness between husbands and wives which can cause insurmountable problems. As I mentioned in my book "Memoirs and Reflections", I have had a few flirtations – a couple before the 1939/45 war, and a few more during the war, but, by <u>my own choice</u> they were all of a strictly <u>platonic</u> nature, but so many cases are reported in the daily press, also radio and TV, which offer gruesome accounts of marital problems, sometimes leading to murder of one, or both people and sometimes any children within a marriage, either <u>losing</u> their lives, or being traumatised for the <u>rest of their lives</u>.

Looking at the world-wide scenario, there is no way in which all its problems can possibly be examined, but I offer a few examples which fall into some of the characteristics as defined in the dictionary, namely <u>"madness"</u> "self importance" or "desire for <u>grand scale</u> action".

<u>MADNESS</u> – starting with one or two historical events – firstly, a little bit about the life of King Henry VIII – this well-known monarch ordered the beheading of two of his wives – Anne Boleyn

and Catherine Howard, also Cardinal Wolsey, and the Earl of Surrey, mainly over quarrels with the Roman Church. In addition to the forms of punishments described above, during the earlier Roman control of this country, punishment of Christians could be for them to face the lions in an arena – as a spectacle!

Oliver Cromwell (a Puritan) fought the Royalists (English Civil War) – he deposed King Charles I, and ordered his execution. Other "mad" events are such things as quarrels between nations – the motive is often for the "power" enhancement of their leaders, - examples, the USSR (Russia) threats against both Chechnya and Ukraine, or Israeli quarrels with Islamic states (Iraq, Iran, Syria) about the State of Israel, also continued skirmishes over Gaza, Lebanon etc; cultural examples – UK and Ireland (difference of religion); Greece and Turkey, over the ownership and occupation of the Island of Cyprus, and the final example in this category, - the vicious quarrel between two tribal cultures, the Hutu and Tutsi tribes in Rwanda (Africa), in which the Hutus slaughtered about 800,000 Tutsi over tribal differences. (I think the date was in the late 1990's). Still ongoing – cultural difference and slaughter in Sudan.

In this "madness" classification, surely the following examples between <u>individuals</u> must be included. The first being paedophiles (many elderly males) violating young girls from 2 to 3 years of age and into teenage – there are so many cases, that I will not attempt to delve any further, except to say that there have been recent cases of <u>young</u> paedophiles violating <u>very elderly ladies</u> = gross malevolence! Lastly, cases of male paedophiles visiting a foreign country to feed their horrible habit! Some of these vile individuals have developed this as a way of life, but there are many cases where alcohol and drugs lead people into evil ways.

Drug taking has led to recent reported cases of prostitution, simply because the young women "needed" money for drugs. The cases of murder of five prostitutes in Ipswich in December 2006 fall into this sad category.

Other thoughts on the madness theme include the vacuous stupidity of certain sections of spectators at football games. It probably takes the silly action of a small group, to cause it to quickly spread to larger groups. Reasons vary – some blame a referee for making a wrong decision, some taunt a member of a different race in the opposing team or a bad foul committed, etc. At occasional games, trouble can continue <u>after</u> a game. There are also some players who play at a furious and challenging pace. Managers and coaches should clamp down on such practices – <u>some</u> do, but often a "blind eye" is turned! And such offences continue. It spoils the game for spectators enjoying an otherwise competitive game.

SELF IMPORTANCE – two or three examples in this section. Who makes the rules for the citizens? President Mugabe of Zimbabwe is a prime example. His policy of taking away the thriving of farms run by white farmers, and giving them to members of his coloured population. Their inexperience in farming has led to perilous shortages, which also massively adds to his debt-ridden regime. At present, in millions of pounds of deficit! Even at this time, Mugabe has been given a further two years to remain as President to avoid a competitive election for this office which is due shortly. This continuation was announced in December 2006. He has already been the President since 1987. Incidentally, the inflation in Zimbabwe has phenomenally risen, and the low wages paid to citizens is <u>totally inadequate.</u>

From 1933, Adolf Hitler boosted his power to wage a cataclysmic war (which became world-wide) to regain forfeited territory. Fidel Castro has ruled as a Communist dictator in Cuba, and his population has been held in humble compliance throughout his reign from 1957 to the present time (December 2006). Recent reports have indicated that his life may be drawing to an end.

Also under this self-importance section, one can point to the way many Chairmen and Directors of large companies, in both this country and the U.S.A who consider themselves as all-powerful! Many of these officials act with excellence, but some feel the can "get away" with fraudulent trading; a few are judged guilty and end up serving a prison sentence. Examples, - a large U.S.A. company, ENRON, had some of its top officials judged fraudulent in a Court of Law, and are now in prison. A recent example in the U.K. was the fraudulent trading of a Christmas saving scheme - FAREPAK, when thousands of clients regularly saved during the year (2006) totalling £80 million, but defaulted in paying it back (due to misuse of the savings). Rescue packages attempted to help with paying it back, but were only able to raise a pittance of about £5 million.

Punishment for the dishonest offenders (at December 2006) has still to be enacted because the crooked dealer fled abroad, and are still to be apprehended and charged with fraudulence and to serve some punishment.

Other cases could be quoted, but there is also the sense of self-importance among political leaders of all political parties. Often many almost insurmountable problems arise as a result. (e.g. Margaret Thatcher – council tax and public dissension which it aroused, and Tony Blair – Iraq war and "weapons of mass destruction" debacle).

I will mention just one other example of a kind of importance displayed by "bossy" awkward people who attempt to dominate others people- sometimes referred to as "Neighbours from Hell" – they create misery to a good many other people.

"GRAND SCALE" DISPLAY – Many so-called celebrities – film stars, TV personalities, footballers and very rich business men/ women, seem to have "money to burn", and whatever they do, it is done on a grand scale. Recent examples are the wedding of Katie Holmes and Tom Cruise, when over £1 million was spent on the ceremony (one other alleged amount was £5 million!), but no doubt newspapers guessed this figure for the purpose of a "good headline". The marriage of Catherine Zeta-Jones and Michael Douglas a year or so ago (probably about 2003/4) was said to have cost £2 million.

The very high wages of footballers (plus lucrative sponsorship deals!) are evident by the way in which they are reported to spend vast sums of money to "enjoy" their leisure time. Recent divorce cases of rich celebrities have referred to very large sums of money as part of a settlement deal.

I will attempt to put these happenings into some kind of perspective. To do this, I will describe a report I read about many years ago (approximately mid 1960's), in which a team of scientific investigators in the U.S.A. set up an experiment to study the effects of living in crowded conditions. They prepared an enclosed space which was reasonably sizeable enough space to enable a pair of rats, male and female, to live a comfortable life. They regularly supplied them with sufficient food and drink, made certain that warmth and air space were adequate. Being a mating pair, it was not too long before a litter of young rats appeared. Still supplying all necessary food and drink, etc, the off-springs also developed and began breeding until the whole enclosure became a profusion of heaving bodies. At this stage, the main study began.

It was noticed that the activities of this mass of living creatures dramatically changed. There were cases of <u>aggression</u> between the rats; some <u>retired</u> quietly at the corner of the compound, and became "drop outs"! Such was the lack of space that any movement by the rats necessitated crawling over the backs of the others; <u>defiant</u> behaviour was noted, inasmuch as some male rats were attempting to mate with other males, as far as could be ascertained, small groups appeared to be led by a <u>dominant</u> leader.

As the experiment was conducted with <u>animals</u>, it could not be completely compared with human beings, but it appears that living in overcrowded conditions <u>may</u> affect <u>human</u> life.

Some of our towns and cities are very overcrowded, also many functions <u>attract crowds</u>, and it is possible to conclude that it may have some bearing on the behaviour of human activity, but, of course, there are many other reasons. Certainly quarrels between people can be aggravated (it even happens in small family situations), and within crowds can be more likely when "spurred on" by others, and, as with the rats example, some <u>look</u> for some kind of <u>leadership</u> (the "bad" often dominates!) Less crowded conditions do not necessarily solve these problems. <u>Leadership</u> by parents is <u>vital!</u> Children are then guided in their early lives, which sets a pattern of behaviour. A quote by a distinguished leading public figure has stated "Give me a child for the first seven years of their lives, and I will give you the <u>man/woman</u>."

The population of the world (now nearly 7 thousand millions) is still growing fast in some parts of the world – China, with a population approaching 1100 millions, attempted to keep down their population by married couples being permitted <u>two children only</u> (the two replacing the two parents after they die), thus not adding to the population. On the other hand, economies like our own country needs a family of between 2 and 3 children (hence the proverbial 2.4 children!), to ensure that an up-and-coming working population creates funds, via taxation, to look after the needs of the elderly, (social, cash, medicines etc.)

Countries need good leaders whether political, or those of <u>competent</u> self importance are a prime necessity, which may garner their lives for "grand scale" existence – altogether something of a mad metaphysical thought!

But, what about the question of increasing population of the world? Some countries still have room for expansion; in a country like ours, space is greatly restricted for housing, transportation, food production, burial space and industrial growth. It will be years before it creates an impasse, but already space exploration has set minds wondering about the possibility of "life in space"! – An impossible dream? – it seems so, but until the 1960's, having a man <u>landing</u> on the moon looked like an impossible <u>pipe-dream</u>, So?? – <u>Never say never!</u>

Narrative 21

<u>WHALES AND MINNOWS</u>

The title suggests the extremes of size, and it is with this in mind that I wish to make a few comparisons.

Towns like Kettering, and many, many others, have developed at a pace which is governed by the size of its population, also people living in surrounding areas. As well as making provision for dwellings to house the people, there must be the growth of all the day-to-day needs of individuals, - roads, schools, banks, doctors, police, legal practices, churches, hospital facilities and much more. The regular needs for shops, or markets, are also vital, and if we think about how these are provided, it is almost certain that in early development, there were many small traders and shops. As these businesses grew, so their size increased either by expansion, or by being "taken over". Thus, town centres grew accordingly, also the spending power of growing populations, and main town shopping centres developed – still many local traders, but also the initial encroachment of national companies.

Part of this huge growth introduced names of well developed reputable companies like Woolworths, Marks & Spencer and many more, as well as the national postal service – the Royal Mail, with its main office and many small sub-offices. At one time there were over 20,000 in the UK – now down to 14,000 and consideration at present for the closure of up to another 4,000 (announced in December 2006). Further changes came about with growth of specialist traders, such as Comet (electrical appliances) Halfords & Currys (vehicle accessories and domestic electrical goods), Debenhams, Next, Dorothy Perkins (ladies fashions), Argos (wide range of household goods), also Banks, Building Societies, Estate agents, Solicitors etc. these grew in size according to the needs of the community, but, from about the 1960's a new phenomenon manifested itself – the <u>Supermarket</u> – initially mainly trading with grocery commodities, and, because of their size, were able to bring in large bulk quantities (for their many shops around the country), and could also pressurise their suppliers to accept the lowest possible payment for the goods, and therefore could pass this on to their customers in lower prices- all very good for the buying public!

In the early days of their appearance, one of them – J.Sainsbury's grew from <u>one small shop</u> in <u>London to become the largest</u>, but have since been overtaken by Tesco, although Sainsbury's has shown good signs of improving profitability, as at years 2005-2006.

There has also been another pressure from an American Company – Walmart, which also combined with UK's Asda to make a very large competitor, and as well as prices, they are all being more conscious of quality of both goods and service. This all seems to measure up as "good for the public", but there is much more to consider, other than price and quality. I neither praise nor besmirch the trading methods of these "Whales". A similar large trader is the Co-operative Movement, and they are, in some respects, larger than the ones already mentioned, as they are owners of their own farms, and there is also a manufacturing base for large range of goods. All of these are run under the rules laid down by the Co-operative Union, and are also under the watchful eye of locally elected committees which would be critical if the standards of their own employees' conditions and wages/salaries were below legal standards laid down. In no way do I suggest that other supermarkets do not pay regard to workers' conditions and earnings, but the structure of the Co-ops is such, that they do not "pay over the top" for the General and Departmental managers, and they are not on the same earning bracket as the enormous ("fat-cat") payment as made by the private sector to their management staff.

I have intimated elsewhere that large salaries may be justified to obtain the experience needed to be good managers, but the gap between managers and workers is much larger than in the Co-operative enterprises.

There are 5 main areas in which I am critical of the large, privately owner superstores.
1. Shareholders would protest vehemently if their managers allowed their profits (thus the shareholders' dividend) to fall

if the business did not <u>continue to grow</u>, so the management teams are always looking for new areas of growth. Profit margins in the grocery trade are <u>relatively small</u>, and these giants are always looking for more lucrative markets, thus they have branched out into such things as wines/spirits, or household items like freezers, washing machines; televisions and many other electrical items – radios, DVDs, computers, etc.

More recently they have moved into banking, insurances, mail order products, tourism, children's and simulations of ladies' top fashion garments and many other goods and services. All these additional sales <u>compete</u> with the many established types of businesses, and the profusion of these form the pattern of trading in our <u>town centres.</u>

There are no appointed Directors in the Co-operative enterprises, but a local committee (very meagrely paid) elected by the members, and from the outset traded in <u>all</u> commodities that people needed.

2. The demise of some town centres has already begun, and whilst I know that there will not be a complete change in my lifetime there is no doubt that town centres will gradually be denuded of the present range of shops, and people will be denied the mixture of these shops.

3. Elderly people and those without their own transport will find it increasingly difficult to do their main weekly shopping for food and a dwindling choice of clothing, shoes, etc, because most superstores are built on the periphery of a town, and cost of taxis and public transport, adds costs to the shopping bill!

4. The power of the supermarkets' buyers to "push down" the cost of goods from their suppliers is a grievous blow to suppliers. An example is those providing <u>fresh</u> milk – the difference of what is paid to the farmer and the price of milk in the store is <u>unjust</u>. Milk is often offered almost as a "loss leader". Even though there are middleman's costs (transport, refrigeration, tests for fat content etc.) to be added, the stores keep their prices at as <u>low a level</u> as

possible (using cheap imported milk if necessary), and it is usually the local farmer who bears the loss!

5. Even when the large superstores provide a number of in town "convenience shops", they in no way make up for the loss of the individual small trader from the town centre. From <u>successful</u> small retailer, <u>larger</u> ones grow (see remarks re: J. Sainsbury above).

To finalise these thoughts, I cannot see how any "control mechanism" would be possible – it would maybe possibly help if they expanded their business overseas, which some have done, but I suspect that because of the voraciousness they display, they would want growth both at home <u>and</u> overseas!

A reverse situation can be seen with a present "Whale" – the Royal Mail, which has announced the possible closure of many of their sub-offices. For many years there were 17,000 (20,000 until reduced to this number) sub-offices throughout the UK, but now down to 14,000 and a present demand to close up to another 4,000! This is bad news for villages in rural areas, which look upon these loss-making offices as a kind of bank (the <u>main banks</u> are also moving out of such areas due to their poor customer use). Even though postal costs are much greater since October 2006, they are, in the main, in line with other world postal services. Perhaps the Government could permit <u>one extra penny</u> on all postal charges, and this, (if "<u>ring-fenced</u>"), and used for <u>no other purpose</u>, could allow grants to cover the rural losses, that is, the <u>general public</u> providing a life-line to its smaller less successful offices. I believe that it is vital to keep all the postal facility serving <u>all</u> areas. Some of these are often the main centre of activity.

As stated above, the rural post offices have considerably reduced in number. Now private companies are permitted to compete with the Royal Mail, but they are very <u>selective,</u> and only handle the bulk type of deliveries (the reasonably easy and profitable type) but our main service are <u>legally required</u> to collect letters and packages from the remotest part of the country, and to deliver them to <u>all parts</u> of the UK, even the remotest areas.

Public Transport at one time was required to handle all the goods and passengers when it was <u>regulated</u>. Once de-nationalised the regulations were cancelled, and all manner of private services, only served the profitable routes, when sometimes one of the two buses went to pick up passengers from the same bus stop, and on other occasions there were none when needed. As at present, (December 2006) there is a call for bus services to be <u>regulated again</u> and I am certain that, like the regulated London Red buses, it will provide a much more reliable service.

Regulate the "Whales"?? – I am not sure, but unless some kind of steadying control is initiated, shopping for some will be a "nightmare" in the distant future.

Narrative 22

<u>WARTIME THOUGHTS</u>

(Not in chronological order)

1. Ration Books issued about three months after war was declared - all basic food commodities (introduced at intervals until 1942). It covered such items as bacon, ham, sugar, butter, meat, tea, margarine, cooking fats, and cheese, followed by jam, marmalade treacle and syrup. Also in 1941, eggs, and then milk distribution was controlled. In 1942 sweets were rationed (points allowed in Ration Book), and finally just a few months after the end of the war, bread was rationed (1946-1948). All these items were de-rationed as food supplies became available, and by mid 1954, there was no more rationing.

2. Whilst all service personnel were issued with their own special <u>gas-masks,</u> the remainder of the population (men, women and children) were fitted with their own mask, which was housed in a cardboard box (approx. 6" cube, with a cord attached), so that it could be <u>carried at all times</u>. It was a black rubber face mask, with a transparent section to enable a person to see where they were going, and a round filter unit to coincide with the nose and mouth. These were individually fitted, and as stated, had to be with you wherever you went! A lot of people hated them, but I suspect that in the case of an emergency (which did not happen!), they would have been accepted as a life-saver!

3. Many homes had <u>no telephone </u>(mobiles not invented). Quite a lot of people tried to get a phone, but they were <u>very</u> slow to be installed, and some 'shared' a line. If one of these sharers engaged in long conversations, or were business people, the other partner had long waits for the line to be cleared!

4. As the war progressed, <u>immediate</u> news relied on the radio. The next editions of newspapers added more details, and (if possible) the odd photograph to illustrate (there were few televisions). Cinema newsreels (Movietone, Universal etc.) provided follow up pictures as part of their programmes, but these were often <u>weeks</u> later.

5. Kettering factories (clothing, boots and shoes and engineering) and kindred trades were fully occupied supplying the needs of the armed forces.

6. A National Register and simple <u>Identity Cards</u> were issued to all people by the end of September 1939.

7. As materials became less available, clothes for the civilian population brought about <u>"utility"</u> clothes, footwear etc. These were rationed by clothing vouchers, and recognised by the "CC" symbol. Ladies' skirts could only be knee length and without pleats or flares. Mens' clothing restricted - jetted rather than flap pockets, nor more than one inside pocket, no PTU's (permanent turn-ups) on trousers. (See "NEW LOOK" post war fashion in later notes).

8. Food shortages needed many "mock" recipes by housewives. The Ministry of Food (Minister Lord Woolton) issued many recipes to make as good meals as possible with limited ingredients and much use of "left-over's". Many surprises in <u>"food queues"</u> - people joined any/every queue to get what was available - unsure of whether it would be bananas, tomatoes, oranges etc.

9. There were very few motorcars, and those being used were subjected to petrol shortages.

10. There were only very odd televisions in use, - the surge of new models did not commence until the early 1950's.

11. As mentioned, radios kept people informed of any news items - much news in early years of wars was <u>bad </u>news. Comedy shows like ITMA (Tommy Handley) were very popular - many gathered round radio sets to listen! It provided light relief during harsh times!

12. Great shock caused by German air raids of many cities - Coventry, Plymouth, Sheffield and many others, particularly those making arms, ammunition etc.

13. The <u>blitz</u> (short for blitzkrieg - German word meaning <u>intense</u> and <u>violent</u> attack) of London leading to the Battle of Britain, - when the "few" airmen (in Spitfire and Hurricane fighter aircraft), took on the force of many hundreds of German bombers. <u>Many</u> aircraft were destroyed. In total the German losses were so great that Hitler drastically reduced the raids - Winston Churchill's rallying war time speeches, included the well known one praising the "few" (British airmen) for their successes.

14. British sense of <u>retribution</u> when, on many occasions, people heard the incessant drone of hundreds of our aircraft which flew overhead on the way to bomb German cities.

15. Kettering itself was not badly bombed, but I think something like two or three bombs were dropped, causing some damage to property, and incendiary bombs landed in Dryden Street and partially destroyed a small warehouse. There were one or two reports of German airmen (probably one or two) whose bodies were found in the area.

16. Many naval tragedies with the loss of naval battleships, troopships and merchant ships sunk by German U- Boat submarines - great loss of both ships and life!

17. Eager radio listening when our North African Army (The Desert Rats) began to drive the Germans out of Africa, through Italy and advancing towards Germany. (Many heavy battles in Italy).

18. Much eager radio listening after the D-Day landings in Northern France in May 1944.

19. Eagerness extended as USSR troops drove the Germans <u>westwards</u> and Britain and Allies drove them <u>eastwards</u> in the "race to Berlin".

20. Delight in June 1945 with the defeat of Germany.

21. Much celebration and <u>many</u> street parties (in spite of food rationing!)

22. It was not too long after war ceased, and materials began to be more available, that the fashion-trade persuaded the ladies to go for the "New Look" - calf length skirts with full flaring.

Narrative 23

JAW OR WAR?

Throughout the world's recorded history, there have been innumerable accounts of wars between an assortment of tribes, mobs, clans and other conglomerates, as well as those between major countries for such things as political or religious reasons. Some start because of trivial disagreement leading to major conflicts.

Those of our countrymen and women who are at present nearing the age of 100 years may still be able to reflect on the horrors of the First World War (The Great War), and this was declared to have been "the war to end all wars", but this was certainly not the case! At the end of this dreadful hostility in 1918, the Treaty of Versailles was enacted, which led to the victors (Britain and troops from the Empire, together with assistance from the USA), confiscating parts of the victims (Germany) territories, to deter further conflict. This was not to be!

At the end of the 1920's, there was a world financial crisis, brought about what was known as the Wall Street Crash of the stock exchange in the USA. This affected not only the United States, but other trading countries - Britain and European countries, including Germany. There was an unabated loss of trade, leading to prolonged unemployment in all these nations. This seemed to be beyond the wit of politicians to solve in all of these countries.

Just over a decade after the end of the Great War, (late 1920's - early 30's), saw the rise of a German political figure - Adolf Hitler - (birth name was Scheikelgruber). His message to the German people was that he would end unemployment of his country's workforce - they could scarcely believe him, - but he was duly elected to supersede the Kaiser, and he assumed the title of Chancellor in 1933, - and then took action!

He used all available resources to build up military strength -

employed people to manufacture a naval fleet of battleships, cruisers, destroyers etc; enforced the production of guns, bombs, tanks, and other armoured vehicles, together with ammunition; ensured the manufacture of very many hundreds of aircraft, - bombers, fighters, reconnaissance craft, etc. He also recruited the personnel to man this weaponry. By this process he <u>certainly got rid of the unemployment</u>, but now possessed such military might that it would serve no useful purpose unless it could be put to use.

On the strength of this change of fortune, most German people regarded him as a kind of saviour of the nation, and this added to his strength. Hitler commenced to expel those who were against his policies, (often by <u>brutal</u> means) until he became the <u>complete Dictator</u> of the German nation and its policies. Meanwhile, the Allied victors of the Great War, still believed the dictum ("war to end all wars"), and many of them, including Britain, pursued a policy of <u>disarmament.</u> Many of our leading Government figures of the time, did not appear to apprehend the possible consequences, in particular in Europe - one almost lone voice, - that of Winston Churchill - made his views known of the menacing dangers which lay ahead, but it was not until the "crisis of Munich" in 1938, that it began to impress British politicians of the probable dangers developing.

Hitler used some of his military strength to occupy a number of those territories which were confiscated from Germany (following the Versailles Treaty) - Alsace Lorraine, Schleswig Holstein - <u>without a fight!</u> Hitler continued to covet Germany's lost territories. With equal simplicity, his troops marched into, and overwhelmed Austria. By this time, European politicians began to see the wisdom of Churchill's warning, and when it was revealed the Czechoslovakia was being viewed as a desirable country to re-occupy by Hitler, our own Prime Minister of that time (Neville Chamberlain) paid a speedy visit to the <u>Fuhrer</u> (as Hitler had taken as a title) in an attempt to "negotiate" with him to prevent the invasion of Czechoslovakia. With the agreement of Hitler (together with France and Italy, Hitler gave his word that if he was allowed to occupy that country, free from any objections from Britain and these other states, he (Hitler) would have <u>not further</u> territorial objections - <u>some promise!</u> Chamberlain flew back to Britain and, waving a piece of paper when he got off the plane, declared that he believed he had secured "peace in our time". So Czechoslovakia was sacrificed.

By this time, Britain, in particular, began to make some preparation for a conflict. A Parliamental Order was passed which decreed that <u>all those male persons reaching the age of 20 years,</u> would be <u>conscripted</u> for 6 months <u>National Service</u> and this would be of a military nature.

There was a choice of the army, navy or airforce. (A small number of these people claimed to be <u>conscientious objectors),</u> but they were interrogated, in <u>very</u> great depths. If they did not serve militarily, a place would be found for them serving in a <u>Coal Mine!</u>

Some of my friends discovered, (and tried to persuade me) that if we chose to serve the local Regiment (Northants Yeomanry) by regular weekend training, and a couple of weeks camp as part of this training, one could be excused conscription. Those who chose this route, found that, by the beginning of the Second World War (Sept. 1939), they were well enough trained to be <u>immediately</u> sent out to stand against the German troops, on the western side of the French Maginot Line, - the so-called "impervious defence" and the Germans were preparing to overwhelm Europe itself. Full conscription was made affective by 1939.

Hitler of course, <u>reneged</u> on his promise about "no further territorial claims", by marching into Poland, and because be would not withdraw; it was declared that a "state of war" <u>immediately</u> existed between Germany and Britain, which also included other European countries.

Conscripts who chose the weekend form of service instead of the 6 months block training, were those who, later, suffered the tragedy of the Dunkirk evacuation. I say tragedy, but by gargantuan effort, over 300,000 British troops were evacuated (-under fire!) and returned to Britain. They went straight back into their own units, and after a few recuperative weeks, were made ready for their next military engagements.

Alliances were formed during the war, for examples the USSR (Russia), also Japan after Pearl Harbour attack, was considered as an ally, after Hitler sent a large number of his armies there in order to conquer this vast country, but it turned out to be a big mistake; - the surprise at the <u>strength</u> of the Russian forces, together with the <u>intense winter conditions,</u> and the long lines of communication needed for supplying food, ammunition, plus warmer clothing etc. These proved to be Germany's stumbling block, and their retreat from Stalingrad continued until the end of the war, coupled with the Allied forces' triumph in driving Hitler's troops out of North Africa, through Italy and on towards Germany, and completely annihilated them, - but then, - another "war" (the Cold War) - Russia's desire to take control over the thoughts and strength of the European countries. This situation gave rise to one of Winston Churchill's great wartime speeches - "Jaw, Jaw is better than War, War"- in other words <u>negotiations</u> rather than <u>bloody battles!</u> - But Russia refused!

There have been other war zones for example Japan and the Far East, after the Pearl Harbour attack brought in the USA, The Falklands, Iraq etc., which cannot be divorced from local memories. Many friends from this area and many accounts from these people form the basis of this book.

Narrative 24

THEY CALL IT "PROGRESS!"

Human lifestyle on planet earth follows a pattern of development, starting from a primitive existence, to one which is more comfortable through the discovery and evolving use of equipment, which is designed to reduce the drudgery of repetitive needs. This process is always ongoing due to mankind's desire for betterment. This goes together with the pattern of conformity by the people according to which "class" they accept is the one of which they acknowledge they are part.

Another influence is that of regulation. Like rules set out for a game of sport, (without which its pursuance would be confused and pointless!), life needs its regulation, to prevent, an otherwise, tangle of problems. This, in a democracy, is ordered by the selection and election of individuals to set the rules (the Law).

During the time that Britain was in its primitive stage, there were a number of other countries in the world, which were civilisations already steeped in the riches of art and culture. Some of these countries were small, for example Incas, Aztecs and Maya territories in the North Western area of South America (in the area between Mexico and Peru). Other larger cultures were the Chinese Dynasty, Mongolian Dynasty (India) - The Moguls, Egypt, Ottoman Empire (part of the Turkish Dynasty), the Greeks and the Romans.

Throughout its existence, Britain was subjected to many invasions, such as the Saxons, and the Scandinavian countries, - the Danish Vikings (traders and pirates), Norsemen, etc. There were also raids from Italy, the Romans, who invaded before the birth of Jesus Christ, and again in years following. Part of the Roman culture was very practical in nature, and their innovations included the building of a network of roads, many,(with updating), are still in use today. They also applied their skills by using a kind of concrete, to construct many buildings with their own style of architecture, also defences - (Hadrian's Wall) the social use of water (the Baths) incorporating a system of plumbing. They also had a form of Government, with a Senate (the governing council), and Consuls (the magistrates), which probably set a pattern of our own form of government. Also the Norman Conquest in 1066AD and their influence was also extremely important.

Beside all these invaders from other lands, the indigenous groups of Angles, Picts, Scots, Welsh and Irish regularly quarrelled with each other, leading to wars which established the four separate countries. Eventually there was agreement to become the United Kingdom (starting with Scotland in 1707 AD), and the Union Flag (Union Jack) incorporated the flags of each. A dissent followed in the early 1920's, and the southern part of Ireland broke away and was first called the Irish Free State, and finally named Eire. The remainder of the four original states - England, Scotland, Wales and the Northern part of Ireland, became known as the United Kingdom (or the UK). Even today (2007), some Scotsmen and women wish to separate and be free from the rule of UK Parliament.

Britain went through phases of development, - the Dark Ages (approx. 500-1000AD), Middle Ages (approx. 1000-1453 AD) and the Renaissance (14th - 16th centuries), when art and literature were revived throughout Europe (influenced by classical forms).

The major change of Britain came with the development of industry, early in the 19th century. It became known as the Industrial Revolution. Yarns, previously spun on hand-operated spinning wheels, were transformed by the invention of the "Spinning Jenny", which was capable of much faster yarn production. This was quickly followed by the invention of a hand-loom capable of weaving materials much faster, and speedier still, after the application of an engine driven by steam power, (developed form George Stephenson's steam engine) in the early 19th century. All these developments followed logically by various inventors of the time, and industrial production in Britain led the world, and incidentally provided employment (taking many people from the traditional farm work) even though wages were quite pitiful, whilst the mill owners began to form the "rich elite" of the country. It was not too long before other countries copied the same ideas, and <u>competition</u> started between them.

Progressing from these early developments, Britain, since that time, has always been conscious of trying to maintain its productive strength. There are many <u>well-paid </u>industrial managers to do this!

That was a <u>very brief </u>"potted history" of Britain's development, but, what about our competitors? The United States of America started their development after subduing the native Indians and taking their land for their own use. Christopher Columbus (Italian) is credited with discovering the expansive "new world" in 1492, although others explored the coastal areas (e.g. Amerigo Vespucci, (another Italian) and his name gave rise to the name America. In 1620 AD, the Plymouth Pilgrims sailed from Britain and a little over seven weeks later, first set foot on this new continent, and many other emigrants followed, in particular the enormous influx of the Irish at the time of the destructive potato famine in 1845 AD. In its early days, America was under the rule of Britain as a colony, but dissent about the payment of taxes, led to a violent protest in 1773. It was known as the <u>Boston Tea Party</u>, and the country broke free of Britain. They laid out a new written Constitution, which directed peoples' activities, and, with great emphasis on education, produced many potential managers, scientists and entrepreneurs and this quite quickly established a powerful industrial base.

For many years, the USA supplied much of the world with goods, services and food, and was the world's number one trading nation, but other countries, (whilst providing a small percentage of world trade), have, of recent years, shown signs of enormous growth. To mention two countries - the USSR (Soviet Russia) and China, - both these existed under a <u>Communist</u> regime. Whilst communism was intended to make a living with some kind of <u>equality</u> between all people, - that was just the <u>theory</u> of it. The practicality is that, if someone is expected to take a large degree of responsibility, they expect to be compensated by a higher income, and that, together with a good deal of the top leaders getting <u>much higher </u>rewards, brought about much dissatisfaction. This was held in check by a high degree of policing, and security personnel, ensuring that too much grumbling was kept <u>very muted.</u>

Russia has just reported the death of a former President, - Yeltzin (year 2007), who, following the previous President - Gorbachov (who began to ease the grip of communism), allowed Yeltzin to take the credit of ending it! The result is that, whilst there is a long way to go to set it up a good capitalist system of free enterprise, a start has been made, and quite a number of previous communist industrial managers, are now in the "millionaire bracket" - there is still much poverty, but changes are afoot, and more and more goods will come from Russia.

The second country - China, also a former Communist country (world's largest population), now has a very fast growing industrial base, and because of its "cheap labour", can now mass-produce and supply a profusion of goods of all descriptions. Countries like Britain have seen almost the demise of some industries (clothing and footwear in particular), because wholesalers and large retailers can import such needs at very low prices. China, then, is a force to be reckoned with!

Another large country, - India - a former country under British rule, until Mahatma Gandhi (the leader of the Nationalist Movement), opposed such rule by silent protest in the early 1940's. It was not until his death (assassinated by explosion in 1948), that India and many other former Empire countries were given the independency to rule themselves in the 1960's. Changes began slowly, but during the 1980's and 1990's, there has been a big surge in the growth of industry and commerce.

India has been hindered by the caste system. There are four main castes - the Brahmin being the highest and mainly for the priestly group. The other three, graded according to the status of each, and finally the lowest - the "untouchables" (now renamed the Dalits), but this group do all the undesirable dirty jobs, and they, and their families never get out of it. Although a newspaper report (in May 2007) described that one of the Dalit group, successfully set up his own business, with early difficulties of getting any higher caste members to mix with these lower castes in its early stages until the success of the business gradually overcame the problem. It is possible that a handful of Dalits can raise their status.

The Punjab, mainly Sikh area of India in the North-West region of the country, was renowned for the growing of almost all the food that was needed, but the growth in <u>parts </u>of India is leading to a changing way of life, and now has <u>many millionaires,</u> and quite a lot of food is now imported into India - even though there is <u>still much poverty </u>among its large population (second largest population).

The official language of India is Hindi. Many can converse in English, even though it is not always perfectly expressed.

Much of the Hindu population is in the northern parts of India, and quite a lot of Muslims live in the more southern areas. The two religions do not always easily mix. Many rich and successful Indian business Proprietors <u>say daily prayers </u>to their Lord Ganesh, and believe that Ganesh brings them more success!

Now for a final look at the vast continent of Africa, - much of which relies on gifts or loans form the G8 group of rich countries of the world. Much has been promised by them but they are sometimes slow to comply, but when help is received by these smaller countries, it is <u>not always spent wisely</u>. Much goes on the purchase of arms/ ammunition, etc., to ensure that they have a fighting force "for their protection". In fact, many of these forces ensure that those who disagree with the policies being followed by the country are "kept down". Also, there is considerable dishonesty and fraudulent activity. These countries are often in dispute with their neighbouring states, and quarrels can be costly! Any organisation to offer education is often <u>badly</u> neglected!

Of course, the <u>work ethic </u>is important - there <u>must</u> be the <u>will to want to work</u>. A glance at the regular living pattern and one may obtain a false picture, but <u>it often appears </u>that the womenfolk do much of the regular routine work, and the unemployed men "sit around" with little will to work, although, to be fair, <u>there is a paucity of jobs </u>available.

Some male Africans are good sportsmen (particularly the football fraternity). I am not sure of the spending pattern of these well-paid players, but, like big wage British players, they often <u>do not </u>appear to <u>look to the future</u>. They are a <u>big attraction </u>to the WAGS - (women and girl friends, and sometimes wives), and a lot of their cash seems to be spent on the "good life". Wise players will realise that their playing days are numbered! If they commence at a young age (say 18 years), about 15 years later, in their early 30's, many of them find their lucrative playing days are over! - and, what have they got left?

I do not know what the answer is, but Africa is a very large continent, with a very wide range of climate, and much land. We know that the former Rhodesia (now Zimbabwe) had some thriving farms, providing most of the food needed by the population, with additional crops sold to other countries, and this provided additional wealth. The policy of Zimbabwe has been to turn out the white farmers of these thriving farms, and handed over to inexperienced black citizens. The farms are now unproductive; also the country's inflation is impossibly high (as at 2007 AD).

Whilst I have no solution to these problems, we know from the Rhodesia days, that the land (if well managed), together with the climate could provide good crops, - but of what? The world is on the lookout for crops of oil-bearing quality, as a bio-fuel developing a possible alternative to the fast dwindling fuel oil.

There is vast space, good suitable climate, and it seems to me, worth a thought of developing it, - but who can do it??

Narrative 25

<u>WAR OVER! - THEN WHAT?</u>

I recently listened to an interesting television documentary (May 2007) about conditions in post Second World War Britain. I have no wish to just summarise its context, - I have <u>much more</u> to add. The present generation may find some of it very hard to believe. I will try to relate the story in chronological order as far as I can.

Of course, there was much <u>joy</u> and <u>relief</u> after the signing of the armistice (both Germany and the Far East) was signed, but there were also many grave <u>doubts</u> about what the future held. Reasons for this may become a little clearer after reading this account.

Homecoming for some, both male and female, sometimes created difficulties. The war years gave many opportunities to both sexes to fraternise - some more than others, and upon returning home, they needed to make a decision to impart such information (or not), to their partner. Some may have said nothing, and a trusting wife, or husband would have accepted that life would go on as before. Some <u>may</u> have tried to judge what effect it would have if they owned up to their wanderlust. It may have worked out alright, but it could leave some <u>lasting</u> doubt for ever afterwards! If any pregnancies were involved, how was the relationship amicably ended? Is there any guilt of a man <u>who walks away</u> from a pregnant woman? Was a decision to own up to unfaithfulness serious enough to cause a divorce? Were any older children of the marriage, given <u>any</u> consideration about <u>their</u> thoughts?

So much for some of the personal problems, another decision was necessary. Do they return to their previous job? (Employers were obliged to re-employ them). Do they make a move to some new trade? Would the choice to work away from home be anything to do with any previous restless jaunts?

Industry itself was forced to change. Any of them which

97

could help the war effort, were fully engaged on it. It took a good period of time before it could get back to peace-time production and routines. Some employment was "patchy", making decision more difficult.

All these personal problems were preceded by an event which came as a great surprise to the nation. The war was led in the country by the pre-eminent political "giant" - Winston Churchill. He, by his actions and stirring messages, gave the people confidence, - even in the darkest days of the war years - he was an excellent war-time leader. Imagine his, and the nation's surprise, when the 1945 General Election rejected him and his party for the diminutive stature (and not well-known) leader of the Labour Party, who had never held any full governmental power. The Labour Party only formed in the very early years of the 20th Century - Scotsman Keir Hardie was the first Chairman and Leader. The party had only had a "flirtation" with governing in 1924, and again 1929/31, when Ramsey MacDonald took office as the Prime Minister of a minority government, which had little power to legislate anything of note. In the 1931/35 term, he upset his party's "faithful" by remaining Prime Minister, having appointed a coalition government!

The surprise election result of 1945 was because the war years, together with much unemployment and mediocre government before that, brought an overwhelming desire for change!

Attlee's "unruffled" demeanour belied his astuteness; he did not influence people into excitable action, but he was shrewd enough to legislate a few historical and influential Acts of Parliament during his short time in office. I exclude the Act of Nationalisation, which I believe veered as much to the side of regulation, as the private industrialists did by aiming for freedom from restrictions. The Acts which are significant are:-

a) *The National Health Service* - initially free to everyone, but later, part-payment for certain services are now paid for, e.g. Spectacles, dentistry, prescriptions, etc.

b) *National Insurance* (now Social Security) based on W. Beveridges's "cradle to grave" report - a personal "safety net" for everyone. It was accepted in its entirety by Attlee.

c) *Town and Country Planning Act (1947)* - now considered the foundation throughout the world. (Green belts, Town planning, New towns, planned neighbourhoods, Wildlife Trusts, prevention of "ribbon" developments (miles of housing along main roads), Woodlands set aside (e.g. Epping Forest and others), areas of natural beauty, SSSI's (Sites of scientific interest).

d) *National Parks* - areas of natural beauty set aside for public use.

e) *Education Act (1944)* - based on Rab Butler's recommendations.

f) *Establishment of Industrial Estates* to separate industry from housing areas.

All the above Acts are considered to be of great importance to the British public and subsequent governments have respected them, and left them unaltered in the main.

Regard was also paid to architecture and housing. All houses built from 1945 to about 1952, were required to have a floor area (superficial footage) of 1000 superficial feet; an example can be seen in Kettering on the southern side of the Weekley Glebe Road, where some of the first houses to be built after the war can be seen. Subsequent governments reduced the requirement and permitted 950 super-feet, and 900 super-feet. This meant more cramped living space.

Large architectural partnerships planned and produced buildings which they claimed would be less expensive than the traditional brick-built houses, and would make more economic use of land space (which was not immediately available). These new "exciting" concrete, multi-storey, high-rise flats, after not too many years, revealed unforeseen difficulties - whenever the lifts broke down, it meant a stair climb to all in the higher storeys; dingy entrance access (these frequented by gangs "up to no good"); little contact with neighbours (they were not next door, but on the storey above or below); the distance from shops, also the "weighty" shopping to take back up the building (particularly if the lift is out of action); some people expressed the dislike of the higher and top storeys; a degree of fire risk,(particularly those on the upper storeys) to make a safe escape.

This style of housing fell out of fashion and by the 1960/70's, some were vacated and the buildings destroyed.

Some council housing took the form of <u>temporary</u> "Pre-fabs"; the component parts were made in the workshops and taken to, and constructed, on to prepared foundations (with water, gas, electricity and sewerage ready to connect). They could be quickly built, had good washing and toilet facilities, built-in cupboards, plus the added bonus of refrigerators - a luxury only owned by a small percentage of the population. They were intended to last for 15 years, but very many of them continued for much longer period.

In the early stages of the <u>actual</u> war, Britain virtually "stood alone" at the outset, although the USA, for our wartime needs, arranged a unique scheme called Lease/Lend, - a fund which enabled Britain to buy, guns, ammunition, food etc., in adequate quantity, whenever they were needed, but the cost would have to be <u>paid off</u> over the course of years, after the war ended. I believe the final account was paid off sometime in the 1990's.

The Attlee government, having to start paying back the Lease/Lend debt, struck another bad patch, in the cold snow and icy conditions of 1947 - started in January and intermittently continued until late March, - everything was ice bound, with deep snow heaps over much of the country. 90% of the country relied on coal as its major source of energy, but coal stacks were completely "iced-up" and coal was unobtainable in any large quantity, - the consequence was a rapid run-down of industry and commerce and the government ordering a <u>three-day</u> working week. All this set-back caused a slump in trade, and that, coupled with the question of debt, plus, the cost of waging the war, meant that the country was <u>bankrupt.</u> The USA, realising our plight, plus the loss of trading, devised another exceptional life-line, - the <u>Marshall Plan.</u> But our "iron" Chancellor at the time (Sir Stafford Cripps), kept a firm grip on the cash, in spite of Trades Unions believing that their members were worth more! - he kept a very tight budget.

Another set-back for Attlee in the year following the 1947 winter, - the big "thaw" and consequent flooding in many parts of the country.

Attlee had some very bad luck, but, even if the problems of his government were formidable, it would have been for <u>ANY</u> elected government.

Narrative 26

POWER FOR THE PEOPLE

In one of my earlier articles "They call it progress!" - I recorded my thoughts about how human existence was revolutionised after the discovery in our country, of steam power in the early 19th Century, and that this spread widely throughout the world. There was a great surge in the use of energy after the discovery of oil, which, when processed from its crude state, is suitable for engineering uses, heating, transport (petrol, diesel etc.)

In the years following it discovery, oil's major use has been for transport, after the invention of the internal combustion engine (the motor car), also, with the development of the diesel engine (for both road and rail), and for giving it high octane properties to ensure smooth performances for aircraft use. Initially, supplies of oil were abundant, but now, even taking account of any new oil drilling areas, it appears that supplies are quickly diminishing, and at some date, not too far into the future, they will be completely exhausted. Many expert brains have, for some time, been bringing their skills to bear, to find alternative sources of energy, but, up to the present time (2007), we are far too short to "bridge the gap".

There have always been other ways of providing some power, but it is only a fraction of what is needed. The ancient, old windmills, which were common a hundred or so years ago, served their purpose in taking the drudgery away from the grinding of corn; if a running stream or river were nearby, a watermill, using the moving water, could be employed. The modern equivalent of the windmill, are the designated areas on which are constructed many three-bladed windmills which, (if the wind conditions are favourable), provide energy to activate turbines. At their maximum contribution, they only provide a small percentage of our needs. New wind farms (as they are called) continue to be planned and built, but there are often objections by people in areas in which it is planned to locate them.

Another device, using water motivation, has been the experimentation of devices on the sea - wave power - reliant on the undulations of the sea waves. Not usually a great output, and depends on the movement of the sea surface - large movement being needed for the best results; calm waters offers little return. So, weather conditions need to be regular, and right. Other drawbacks of this method - people do not want them near to the beaches; if they are placed too far out at sea, they become a hazard to vessels; they are costly to produce and maintain, and people, given the choice of location, usually prefer them to be sited elsewhere, and the total of power produced is not great.

Another more efficient use of water is the hydro-power mechanisms. These can only be used where an adequate supply of water cascades to a lower level (waterfall) - the force of the water pressurising the giant cups round a special wheel, which keeps constantly turning (the ancient water-wheel principle on a grander scale). This is only possible in limited areas in the country. It is an efficient producer of electricity, but all those at present in use still only provide a small percentage of our total requirements.

Coal fired power supplies a large part of our needs, but coal is another natural source, which is not an everlasting source! Another drawback which is complained about is the amount of carbon gases in the smoke which are released when it is being processed. A great deal of work continues to be done in an attempt to "clean up" the smoke gases as they are released, but much more needs to be done.

The use of batteries is a convenient way of storing energy for limited periods, but they make no contribution to add to energy supplies, except extremely small quantities obtained by hand-cranked means, which may provide enough for short-term hand-held lights or a portable radio.

Solar power use is being considered more often now. The modern approach is to employ solar panels, either for single buildings, or as a collection of panels, and these gather the heat form the sun, and, depending on its strength and duration, partially heats water which then needs less power to fully heat it for direct use or central heating.

There has been experimentation in the use of hydrogen over many years. Whilst it still needs a great deal of further study as to its safety in use, it has been used successfully as a source of energy. If this could be developed with safety in mind it could provide a good source of supply. It would need adequate and safe areas for storage. Hydrogen is a colourless gas, - the lightest substance known, - and it forms a small part of the air we breathe.

By far the largest source of energy which can be produced, apart from coal is Nuclear power. Britain has had a small number of stations, and, (as at June 2007), is likely to approve the building of more production plants (despite a vociferous opposition by people who will have them planned to be built in their living area). The production plant itself is relatively safe, certainly more so than those built in the early experimental years, but the huge draw-back is that, after its life use, the dangerous cores (which is central to its use), must be very carefully stored, - probably buried, - for hundreds of years (unless scientists can find some method of neutralising them), so succeeding generations of our people will be left to guard this dangerous residue. Because of this, few people would welcome the building of any new plant "in their backyard".

Another possible source of energy is to use bio-diesel, but that would need large areas of land lost for the growing of food items. I did dare to suggest (in my essay at the beginning of this epistle), that the continent of Africa has much land and a variety of suitable temperatures for areas of bio-fuel growth, but that would only be possible with competent (and willing) staff to produce such crops - which also need to have political stability!

From all the foregoing information, it can be seen that the whole of human creation has become completely reliant on the availability of energy to enable it to exist at the present level of development, and there continues to be the urgent need to seek new ways to keep up an adequate supply. Many assiduous brains will need to be applied to keep their thoughts alive to maintain adequate supplies for us to survive!

One or two final thoughts on this subject. Experiments continue to be made, for example, a small experiment on making an alternative fuel for vehicles, shows that mixtures, including such things as vegetable oils are a possibility, but still a mere "drop in the ocean" of our needs.

Other experiments include extraction and storage of <u>natural gas</u> which may be obtained from large landfill sites from rotting vegetation. I mentioned the use of hydrogen and the experimentation of fuel for both road and rail which are ongoing. All of these last three examples give only extremely limited additional supplies.

Maybe politicians could offer rewards to both individuals and large companies, for any of them expounding important ideas supported by successful trials, also that any scientists who can investigate, or better still, completely counter the problem of the storage of <u>nuclear waste</u>, which would then allow the continued use of nuclear energy without leaving future problems for people somewhere well into the future. Nuclear energy is almost the only one which can supply us with sufficient quantities.

It is vital for the survival of the world and its population to solve such problems and to ensure that we have "POWER <u>FOR</u> THE PEOPLE".

Narrative 27

BEING "ARTY"

I chose this anomalous title for this composition, as I wish to explore the reasons by which my interest in art developed.

As is normal, in my very early life - as soon as I was capable of holding a pencil, or crayon well enough, - I went through the "scribbling" stage, when a page of oscillating lines, was said to be mummy, daddy, a house, a dog etc. etc., but with a greater degree of steadiness, drawings began to resemble a truer picture. Development into copying someone else's illustrations, and another way of getting the idea, is by the use of tracing paper.

I began to take a growing interest in my years at school and I today, (over 75 years ago), remember moments which had some impact, for example, in my early secondary school days, we had a young female teacher (probably her first appointment after she became qualified, and an incident which taught me something new, was when we were doing still-life drawing, and on that particular day, we were asked to draw a cutting from a rose bush - lovely colours, exquisite blooms, etc., although we were doing it as a pencil drawing. Apart from the intricacies of the curling petals, the smaller detail of incorporating the spiky thorns down its stem, I made my representation of them with what I thought looked something like the real thing. This young teacher came round to look at it, and, - much to my surprise - said "that looks like a bit stuck on, - give it some guts!", and with that remark, she took my place at the desk, and, with a couple of deft strokes, turned my effort into one which looked as if the thorn was growing from the stem - realistic! The lesson learned, - be bold, not timid, - it may make the picture more realistic.

A further incident in the same classroom some time later

was when another teacher was illustrating water colour work and on this occasion it was for a background colour wash, using a slanted drawing board. With a brush fully loaded from a pallet prepared with a suitably coloured wash, (in this case a blue tint to represent a sky, starting from the top, the loaded brush was drawn across the edge, and follow - up strokes picked up the bulge of water which had drained to the bottom edge of the first stroke. A second application, still a loaded brush, needed only a touch and a second sweep with the brush, and this was repeated with similar strokes, leaving the pale blue background as the basis for the sky. The thing which needed attention was to guide the wash to steer it clear of other parts of the picture. If this was not done, it could sometimes make the application of colours required for the other features, (trees, bushes, houses, etc.) a little more difficult to apply; so the control of the wash is important, also the careful "mopping up" of the surplus wash at the final, lower edge, using the dry fibres of the brush to do so. The finished background gives a suitable base, which, after allowing it to dry out, other colours can be applied to introduce details, such as clouds for skies, rolling waves, for sea, and different lights and shades to represent hills and hollows etc.

Youngsters, with a box of paints, naturally often use the various colours, by loading the brush directly from each colour tablet without diluting it, and the delicacy of the softer "washes" is lost.

In my class, there was a boy who became very expert at cartoon drawings. He could speedily, with few bold sweeps of pencils, crayons etc., produce a most excellent picture of such subjects as Mickey Mouse, Pluto, Minnie Mouse etc. It was fascinating to see him in action. Incidentally, he was able to use this talent when he first started to work with some artistic organisation.

Another memory which remains very much in my mind is that a well-known local artist produced some excellent oil painting pictures - large sized - which were framed with appropriate gilt frames, and he offered a lot of them to the County's Education Authority, and these could be seen at "eye-level" in a number of school assembly halls. In my school, there was one of a pastoral scene of trees, bushes, grassy banks, etc. In the centre of these was a picture of a small lake, and when looked at from several feet away, it appeared that a bird, (probably a swan), was just rising out of the water with its wings slightly open. To my amazement, the "swan", (when viewed at "close quarters") was represented by just a small "splodge" of white oil paint with a brush as if it was just a <u>casual</u> stroke, - my first encounter with oil painting! Some artists apply oil paint <u>very</u> thickly, and this adds to texture.

Another lesson I well remember, was in junior school, when the teacher illustrated "perspective", by drawing a cube on the blackboard, viewed diagonally, so that the front corner edge, (nearest to you), appeared larger than the two far side corner edges which were farther away. "Now draw that", he said, "to show that you understand it!" I carefully drew my cube, as instructed, but what I did not remember is that perspective applied, not only to the side panels, but also to the top panel surface, and that this also had near and distant edges, and, of course, also needed the application of perspective, and, - would you believe it? - I was punished by <u>three cane strokes</u> on the tips of my fingers! I have <u>never</u> forgotten the lesson! Incidentally, this same teacher, giving us another art lesson, administered another cane punishment on me and for what? - I had three "smudgy" finger marks on my drawing paper! I felt that it was an unreasonable punishment in the circumstances, - but that is how it was in the 1920's. This particular teacher carried a cane around in almost all his lessons! - The <u>deterrent</u> effect!

My interest in painting grew when dealing with <u>colours</u>. There is a <u>vast range</u> of them, all produced from the <u>primary colours</u> - red, yellow and blue for example, blue, mixed with yellow creates <u>green,</u> - but, think of the diversity of this colour, - pale, sage, pea, olive, grass, emerald, aqua, apple, jade, lime, malachite, beryl, bluish on yellow tints, the extremes of the range of a plant's new growth and the dark shades when fully mature, and the full range of the evergreens. All these are capable of being displayed from <u>light</u> to <u>dark</u> shades. The same is true of the blues and yellows and the various mixes of these colours can produce an indescribable range of every imaginable shade. Also, when dealing with these water colours, a <u>dilution</u> by water produces the "barely tinted" shades, also a small addition of black or white will lighten or deepen the colour. Human skin only needs extremely soft colour when depicting a white complexion, on "life" drawing, portraiture, etc.

Another medium is _gouache,_ which contains opaque pigment, which is slightly thickened with gum and honey. Its application is therefore more dense. Charcoal is also used for drawing, especially for quickly produced work.

I have referred to _perspective_. A second important element is _proportion_. If you intend to draw a standard plant pot which is displayed as a model, its depth, related to the top diameter must be correct, otherwise it would look either long and thin, or short and fat - nothing remotely like the real pot. Artists often do a quick check by holding a pencil at arm's length, and by sliding their thumb along to compare both vertical and horizontal proportions.

The final important component is to apply _shading_ to distinguish, and give realism to light and dark areas. It would look completely unfinished if depicting normal conditions. If someone said to me -"it's no good, - I _cannot_ draw!" I would say to that person that if they follow the three things - _proportion, perspective_ and _shading,_ they could (if they tried) present a reasonable "first effort", and after that, _practice makes perfection!_

Repetitive practice is required for this, and any of the other arts, - music, drama, etc. Here I "plead guilty", because I attempted to learn to play the piano (for three years from age 7 to 10), but I _failed_ to _practice_ enough. I have always expressed my deep regret, but all too late! The one blessing I have with both drawing and music participation - I can _appreciate_ the _talents_ and skills of the experts. Take note of their _dedication_ to the art, of course, undertaking such arts at a more leisurely pace can be most _rewarding_ through the _pleasure_ it gives.

At my age (88 years at 2007), and failing eyesight, now prevents me from any serious attempt at portraiture - a special skill to produce life-like expressions and appearance - the slightest wrong move of pen or pencil will quickly cause the loss, or creation of a realistic expression. I just wish I was capable of achieving a recognisable portrait of a person sitting as the model!

Narrative 28

FED TO DEATH

I have taken this theme for contemplation as a result of the newspaper cutting, as it seems that, today, there is a great emphasis on the size young (as well as older people) - the word is obesity!

When I was in my early boyhood in the mid 1920's, the problem was not the same. In those days, many youngsters were more likely to be "skin and bones", or in a malign-case scenario, a child may develop rickets, - a disease based on a deficiency of certain vitamins which would cause the development of deformity, due to the softening of the bones. There could be a number of reasons for poor diets - much unemployment together with poor wage levels, causing limited money for household food; there was less knowledge among the parents of the importance of a good balance of diet; there was less understanding of the make-up of diet, e.g. proteins, carbohydrates (the starchy, sugary content etc.) Quite a number of people today, are conversant with their importance; probably the confusing selection from the range of food from which choices could be made.

Looking back on the kinds of morning "snack" type foods which were quite commonplace in the 1920's (-they sound unbelievable today), - examples - a hunk of dry bread (no sliced loaves at that time), occasionally eaten dry, or made slightly more "palatable" with a smear of margarine scraped on to it; sometimes it was made more acceptable by having a sprinkle of sugar scattered over the surface, or another addition would possibly be syrup or treacle (if affordable). A common addition to the bread was cooking lard, finely sprinkled with salt; in the winter months, if a household fire was available, the bread could be toasted. Other surprising snacks were such things as a raw rhubarb stick, dipped into a scattering of sugar in a saucer; another strange dish was a quantity of sugar in a saucer, mixed with half a teaspoonful of cocoa powder - this made a kind of dry chocolate - if a small quantity of margarine was added, it could become a chocolate spread, and if icing sugar was used instead of granulated, the result would be a smoother quality. All those "delights" are of <u>local</u> origin, - there would, no doubt, be <u>many more</u> from other areas of the country! - What a diet!!

Now allow your mind to think about the difficulties of war-time rationing. In the early months of the start of the Second World War (1939), certain foods were reigned back (due to the difficulty of importing them), and Ration Books were issued (one per person) within hours of the declaration of the war. The foods rationed were red meat, butter, sugar, tea (<u>small</u> amounts of each per person); other items in <u>very</u> short supply (fresh fruit, eggs, coffee, cocoa) were controlled by the system of queuing at shops, in the hope of obtaining small quantities.

A new kind of food presentation found a growing popularity - the "potato crisp". Probably the innovating company in Britain, was Smith's, - two "<u>old</u> pence" per packet, and part of the "fumbling fun" was that, if you wished to flavour them with salt, you had to "shuffle" your fingers amongst the crisps to find a small twist of blue waxed paper containing a generous pinch of it, then "sprinkle and shake" before any eating commenced. This novelty food (if you were lucky enough to possess two-pence!), quickly gained popularity, and quite a number of competitor companies began to share this trade.

As you will realise - that which was rationed was diligently purchased by all to ensure they obtained their share. Also imagine the housewives were "tested" in their ability and imagination to produce meals from these limited ingredients. Many recipes were "mock" productions of the real things! A wartime recipe booklet was issued by the Minister of Food (Lord Woolton), which gave a number of ideas for the making of "mock" ingredients, also how to get the best out of "left-over's".

Parents of about the same age as my parents - born in the 1880's, - followed the pattern of their own upbringing as they learned from <u>their</u> mothers the skills of cooking, and the variety of their meals was <u>good, plain and nutritious</u>, with the occasional treats - such as roast beef and Yorkshire pudding, also very occasionally chicken. The ladies at that time, did not meticulously "weigh out" the ingredients but, by experience, took a handful of this, a pinch of that and the other (few scales were available in any case), but the meals always turned out to an excellent standard. The younger, up-and-coming generations had lessons in cookery at school. Today's generation often find that the teaching of cookery is banned (Health and Safety regulations are responsible - dangers of cuts, burns etc.! One can suspect that employers, such as the Education Authorities, are being more than a little cautious, because of the possibility of litigation against them for anything which goes wrong - accidents, cuts, bruises, burns etc., - much of today's outlook of seeking compensation for a variety of incidents, is prompted by firms of solicitors suggesting that possibility, and suggesting that it is your right so to do, by posing general questions - "Have you been injured?" "Have you tripped over a broken footpath slab?" etc.; then stating that they will make the case in law on a "No win, No fee" basis. Thus there are often "frivolous" claims!

In any case, the modern young housewife has different ideas of what is best. They are often engaged in evening classes, clubs, gyms, etc., and find it more convenient to buy ready-made meals, which need a few minutes in a microwave, and it is an almost immediate meal. This may be alright, but food manufacturers put many additives into their products to make them more attractive and, they say, a better flavour. They also consider its effect on the shelf-life of the product, and all this is done to produce the cheapest reasonable cost (if they are competing with other producers), and sometimes Food Standards Officers "take them to task" for poor quality - they also get inspections for cleanliness standards during the production operations. I do not suggest that they deliberately work in a "slip-shod" manner - far from it - but they must always be aware of the ability and standards of those they employ, (good training is essential!) Some are accused of producing meals which are too starchy, too salty, too fatty, etc. (which a person cooking at home can be sure of the ingredients they use).

A concluding thought - in spite of the shortage of food due to wartime restrictions, by the end of the war and the immediate post-war years, the general health of most people was better than the difficult years which I have described, - this was probably because everyone used the allocation of the rationed items which, on balance, were necessary as part of a good wholesome diet.

It is feared by doctors and dieticians that peoples' choice today of stodgy, fatty, salty foods tend to be heavy, filling indigestible, etc., but are presented in attractive packaging and widely advertised - particularly directed to excite the taste-buds of children, also the prediction of experts that if overfeeding us allowed by some parents, it leads to obesity and that, once that state is reached, it could lead to premature death from heart disease, also a trigger for some forms of cancer. An alarming thought!

Narrative 29

KETTERING "CARNIVAL DAY" MEMORIES

This annual event, helped to add to vital income support for the general hospital in the days before the beginning of the National Health Service, after which it was funded by the taxpayers.

It has always been a rallying point for many local businesses and individual citizens to present novel activities of such things as tableaux, mounted and decorated onto a variety of lorries. Many of the entries were provided by factories, offices, clubs and groups of genuinely interested people.

At my age (88years), my memories go back a long way, and in this short article, I will mention just two occasions which may be of interest, the first was (I think) in about the year 1935, and was the display mounted by the Kettering Rowing Club, (which was active at the time). Their theme was to represent one of the amusements provided by the Thurston family during the Kettering Feast Week, Charles Thurston and his son John. The large roundabout, with a series of large humps and dips around a track, and this carried open seated carriages. These were made more "Grand" by being a curve-shaped main body and a significant carving of the head of a peacock at the front, and a small tailpiece at the other end. The complete roundabout was painted with highly coloured motifs.

The rowing club produced a small version of this, mounted on the back of their lorry, also making the rolling hump track, and this enabled a suitably sized "peacock" carrier, and this was occasionally pushed round the track. The whole tableau well represented the real fairground version. On the top "frilled" canopy (which would normally bear the name Thurston's the carnival version showed the name "Thursty'uns" - no doubt an apt name!

The second occasion was (probably) the year 1936, and that was one in which I took a small part. A group of enthusiasts from Kaycee Clothing Ltd., considered what could be the nature of their entry, and, because we could get access to (and temporarily borrow) an old <u>disused Fire- Engine</u> vehicle which had been used by one of the local small towns, (no ladders etc.), so this became our focus. The petrol engine, itself was said to be unreliable, but the "Kaycee" transport department "tuned it up", and it thus, became the basis of our entry - <u>"WILL HAY AND HIS SCHOLARS - FIRE FIGHTERS"</u>

It took me a great deal of pleading to one of my ex-schoolmasters, to lend us the <u>(obviously very precious)</u> academic cap - the mortarboard, and this, together with a black shoulder-like gown, made "Will" look the part! He sat on the seat next to the driver. The small team of "Scholars" wore light-weight jerseys and shorts. They wore large deep (thick cardboard) collars (which I made), and suitable <u>neck gear,</u> together with rather small school-boy caps, and it made them look a <u>"comical bunch"</u>! They had a little "fun" with a bucket of water and a stirrup-pump (which was occasionally used <u>judiciously</u>). It was a showery day, and the scene was made a little more amusing, as "Will" held a brolly over his head! Ah well - all good fun!

<u>Closing thoughts -</u> carnivals of these earlier times seemed to be more celebratory because there was often the attendance of two, three or more carnival bands which, with rhythmic music, and brightly coloured uniforms, livened up the procession on tableaux, and engendered a happy feeling.

Older citizens may remember the experimental "Mile of Pennies" (old currency). One or two white lines were painted (by means of a machine used to mark out sports pitches) down Gold Street and along High Street, with the invitation for citizens to place pennies along the lines, to be later gathered by authorised officials. I would believe that this was a temptation to any <u>UNTHINKING</u> individual who probably picked up one or two of them for sweets or a drink! An impossible thought in terms of present day activities!

Narrative 30

IDLE THOUGHTS

I set forth these deliberations with no particular direction in mind. If we look at some of the dictionary descriptions of the word "idle", it may divulge the reason why it might be of interest. Some of the words associations with it, are such descriptions as triviality, emptiness, insignificance, frivolity, triteness, gibberish, nonsense, unimportant, etc., and one or two phrases, such as "not worth a straw", "no great shakes", "neither here nor there". The contents of this article will reveal that many of the stories fall into some of these categories, but before I could start on such thoughts, I had to group them I some kind of order.

Much of what I want to describe, dates back to any infant childhood, my boyhood, and my teenage years, so I will commence with some of them encountered while I was an infant. Some will be in the form of sayings, on comfort and fun games. Some are found in simple songs of the time, and some as a kind of tongue-twisting gibberish – but I can assure you these <u>really</u> happened, and are not from a world of fancy!

Parents throughout the ages have tried to bring up their children in ways which help them to understand about life in the matters of education, contentment, a loving relationship, possible dangers to be aware of, the sharing of toys (and life) with others, our environment and other living creatures, and all other aspects of life. Some parents manage this with aplomb, but many others (who themselves are still immature and have never "grown up!") cannot conceive the subtle distinctions needed for a successful life-style, and are not always competent in guiding their young children.

I do not suggest that everything done in the past was successful, - there are many examples of failures, - but I describe one or two of the activities which were common place, particularly after the constraints of the Victorian Era.

Tiny infants were kept amused by such fun games (associated with much rural life), as being held gently but firmly on the knees of a sitting parent (probably the mother!) who softly sung "The ladies go nimma-nim-nim", (with a gentle bouncing movement) "the farmers go trotta-trot-trot, (slightly higher bouncing) "old Johnny comes out with his boots and his spurs, and he goes gallopy, gallopy" (with strong, but safe bouncing). The response by most infants - "more-more" or "gen, again!"

Another country side fun game, the parent sitting with the child sitting in her cupped hands (facing forward). The chant this time was (with appropriate leg crossing movement of the child's legs) "Leg over leg as the fox went to Dover, - when he got to the stile, - up it went over" (repeated whilst the child was safely rolled backwards and forwards into the parent's lap) – always brought a "giggle".

There were many other fun songs, and, of course, a great variety of nursery rhymes were in constant use. There was also much "gobbledygook" spoken by way of keeping older children amused, but before I leave behind the infant stage, all kinds of softly spoken words attempted to soothe a child to sleep – an example, a baby held in a parent's arms (probably myself when I was too young to realise what was happening) – would be lulled by quite meaningless words, - "Sssh, tiddy bom bom" – it sometimes "did the trick!"

What about other gibberish? Here are a couple of examples – "Tee-dee, massa – wee, ranty bungaloor, tiggy, tiggy chop chop!" and the second example – "Ie chie chickerie, chickerie pawny, pim-pom pawny – walla western, Chinese junk!" – Don't look so surprised – it has happened many times before and since, - some by well-known literary authors – example "Jabberwocky" by Lewis Carroll (pseudonym of Charles Luttwidge Dodgson) who wrote "Alice in Wonderland" and "Alice, through the Looking Glass". More recently, in the 1930's, the song "Mairzydotes and dozydotes and liddlamzydivy" was a kind of nonsense song, but explained a little when translated to "Mares eat oats and Does eat oats and little lambs eat ivy". There were many others illustrations which could have been quoted.

In my boyhood, I became a member of a boy scout troop (incidentally 100 years since scouting was founded by Robert Baden-

Powell, in July 1907), and my brother, Bob, (now sadly deceased), was a member of the same troop, and when he was aged about 15 years, that is approximately 1927, a world Scouts Jamboree was held to celebrate its 20th Anniversary, and Bob, and a scouting friend attended it, and I remember them constantly chanting a phrase or two which sounded like "Een garn garboor (3 times repeated) een voo boo" I believe they had been fascinated by it when many of the world's scout troops have their traditional sing-song around the camp fire as part of their rallying tradition. I think the chant is based on the Bantu (Zulu) area of South Africa – the area where Baden-Powell served during the Boer War 1880/1 and 1899 – 1902. I have no idea of the meaning of such words, but they still occasionally come back into my thoughts.

When playing various street games, children could, from time to time, be heard trilling a kind of jingle as a precursor to some game to determine the order of play. It went something like "Eany meany, mineracka, rare eye dominaka, chickeracka, om pom, push". At the end of each jingle, one member of the group was eliminated, until the last one, who would hen be declared "it", that is the dominant player in the game. (There were many, many versions of these words, all for the same purpose).

Thinking about playing in the street, (a rare occasion these days), a family from Wales moved into the area. I remember we got a little excited about new friends, and one of them (I think his name was Mansel) recited, in his Welsh lilting voice, "One H, one E, one R, one E, one F, one O, one R, one D, one S, one H, one I, one R, one E. Those who us who followed the quick succession of words, would have recognised that it spelled out HEREFORDSHIRE. Similarly another Welsh children's puzzle was Mrs D, Mrs I, Mrs F-F-I, Mrs C, Mrs U, Mrs L-T-Y. For those with a reasonable nimble brain, - the word DIFFICULTY.

Still in my boyhood, we were gradually moving out of the influence of the Victorian Era, and it was at a time when, up to that time, it was considered to be shocking for a lady to allow anyone see their ankles! A somewhat daring ditty came out around that time (Fame by today's standards) but it was a small song about a lady's underwear! It goes like this: "I've a little pink petty from Peter, and a little blue petty from John, and a green and a yellow from some other fellow, and one that I haven't got on!" - possibly of Music Hall origins, as indeed was another "masterpiece". "What did the poor little moths live on when Adam and Eve were here? – Adam wore no trousers, - Eve, she wore no blouses" etc. Certainly <u>no</u> poetic classic!, but it raised a few smiles.

In compiling the words of this article, I only recounted those that came back to me easily. I suppose that with some deeper thoughts, and possibly a little prompting, I know that I could have churned out many more whimsical words, but I think I have explained enough to reveal some of the fun created. I am certain that if anyone had some idle moments to review their past years, they, too, would recall many smiles and surprises!

Narrative 31

ONLY SKIN DEEP?

The title of this essay is associated with superficiality – something which does not delve below the surface. This may be an apt description of skin which thinly, but efficiently, surrounds a human body. I will certainly have some thoughts about this, but want to make comments of a deeper nature.

Before I consider this any further, I will mention one or two more facts about the skin itself. It has several layers, - the outside one, the epidermis which sheds flakes of dead cells continuously, unlike a snake, which gets rid of such a layer entirely on a periodic basis. The layer below this is the dermis, which is a living layer, and this is in contact with a complex of units of living matter, - the red blood cells, the nerve cells which provide the stimulating impulse of sensation of movement to the brain and these will indicate pain, heat or coolness, etc. This layer also provides new skin as the body needs it, and has great healing qualities, also incorporates a colourless fluid containing white blood cells, which controls infection (lymph).

Since the social revolution – post 1914-18 Great War, - life among the young population became somewhat more colourful and showy. Evidence of this could be seen as some people, particularly the females began to cover their visible skin with make-up! In the early days of this development, these ladies themselves, painted and powdered their faces, - some with little finesse! I once heard it said (in criticism) that a lady applied such paint and stopped abruptly as it reached her neck, and she gave the impression that, as she prepared herself for a social night out, it appeared as if her final act, was to lift an artificial head and face, and place it onto her shoulders! – certainly not a very natural look.

Over succeeding years, the use of make-up improved and is now, usually applied with more realism. Some ladies use very little, and some, with excellent complexions, use none. It is well used for stage and film actors and photographic models. These are usually applied by professionals. But, - how does one judge beauty? As a result of some flippant remark, a friend of mine (in fact, my manager in industry at the time) remarked "beauty is subjective – even a beetle is beautiful in the eyes of its mother!"

At the present, - certainly from the early 2000's AD, manufacturers of cosmetics vie with each other to command a good market share of the business, also publishers lay stress on the importance (according to them) of body proportions and size of both males and females, also in the world of both food and fashion, aided and abetted by the manufacturers of fashionable clothes. Those who organise fashion shows of women's' clothes, seem to choose "thin as a stick" models on the "cat-walk". The important thing is to sensibly eat a balanced diet.

Everything written about so far in this article has referred to the human physique, but there are other considerations. What about emotions? The senses, also including such things as zeal, ardour, pain, rapture, friendliness and many others. If a person is adjudged to be comely or handsome (male) or attractive, charming or pretty etc. (female), that does not take account of the emotions which, to me, are most important. If I were bold enough to say to a lady – "you are an elegant lady" (and mean it), - the lady may be pleased with such a compliment. If a second or third person said this to the lady, she may feel that she is, in some way, superior, and if, as a result, she became boastful she, to me, would have forfeited the description of elegance. It may also allow her uncontrolled emotions to flourish. This could possibly lead to "looking down" on others – not a good example to members of her family and friends. Wouldn't it be gratifying to live in a world where humans are treated equally?

There is certainly something of great importance which develops (if encouraged) into something deeper than skin-deep!

Narrative 32

THOSE LITTLE "WHITE" LIES!

I thought about the subject of white lies, but had to think of a way to introduce it. The deception of lying is <u>serious misconduct</u>, and to a genuine and upright character, it would <u>never</u> be considered. So, what of "white" lies?

I will start off this account in a light-hearted way, developing it as it proceeds. Many years ago, around the 1930's/1940's a popular waltz-time dance band song had a verse from which is:-

Quote – Be sure it's true when you say "I love you", - it's a sin to tell a lie; millions of hearts have been broken, just because these words were spoken. "I love you, yes I do, - I love you; if you break my heart I'll die, so be sure it's true when you say "I love you", 'cos it's a sin to tell a lie!

Part of another song is:-

Quote – The night was drear and dark, and heaven was in your eyes, the night that you told me, those little white lies.

So, even in earlier times, telling an untruth was considered important enough to sing about in the light-hearted dancing days.

Looking at the serious side of telling a lie, very many lives have been shattered by some rogue elements deliberately wishing to blight the life of someone they consider as some kind of opponent, - in business (financial, seeking promotion, etc); boy/girl friendships; cheating husband/wives; quarrels about a WILL among those involved (relatives/close friends, etc.) of someone who has died; responsibilities among those involved in road accidents; claims made for compensation to Insurance companies; and many other circumstances. All of these indicate <u>dishonesty</u>, and should be vehemently condemned, - society deserves better!

But, what of this other category – white lies?   There is

a dictionary definition for it "a harmless lie – one, held for the sake of politeness". An example might be in answer to a request of a lady saying to a friend (whilst displaying and wearing a new garment or dress, jeans etc.) "Do I look alright at the back?" (No doubt worrying about her hip size). The friend's reply might be a remark, such as – "Your figure is well proportioned, - you do not look overweight" Such an answer may really be true, but could also be a polite "white lie". In any case, it is better than saying "You could do with slimming a little!"

Another purpose of a white lie might be in the case of someone's severe illness, and, with the knowledge that the person's close relatives have been warned of an imminent death (about which you are <u>also</u> aware). In such a case it would be kinder to the one destined to the unhappy fate not to be given a really true answer, which may be very upsetting to them. A little white (diplomatic) lie, I believe, would be entirely appropriate.

As, in the words that were quoted at the beginning of this composition, little white lies may defuse many an awkward situation in male/female relationships – there are often enough difficulties arising in such situations during courtship and marriage, without adding to any problems by telling lies or revealing "secrets" about any cheating!

In my early life, I heard the quotation – "You can be <u>sure</u> that your <u>sins</u> will <u>find you out!</u>" I think that is a very good adage! Is there a moral in it? – I think one might say to anyone who <u>habitually</u> cheats or lies – "You would be better served by <u>breaking the habit!</u> It may save <u>many</u> awkward moments, or serious consequences if you don't!

Narrative 33

UNBELIEVABLE
GLIMPSES OF YESTERYEAR

Among my recorded memories, I have described many activities which, through the passage of time, are gone, and almost forgotten. I would like to revive a thought about one or two others which, by their nature, seem beyond credence.

The first is to describe the way many country folk kept and fed a pig to the point when it became fat enough to kill for food. This was quite a common activity before the Second World War, and was taken up by a few townspeople in the years immediately following the end of the war, because of food rationing which, ended about the mid 1950's.

These home produced pigs were mainly fed by what was known as pig-swill, which was a cheap form of food. Those who kept pigs would ask a good circle of friends to keep any suitable left-over food, etc., also from any shopkeepers who were throwing out stale food. These items were softened by soaking them, and the pigs happily "scoffed" it. Pig-swill was later <u>banned</u> by the government because nobody could verify the quality of it, and could possibly affect the quality of the food it produced. However, quite a number of people did it, and I recall visiting friends of one of my relatives who did so, and they were pleased to show me the side of pig meat, which was hung in a darkish pantry. The <u>complete surface</u> of the skin of the pig was covered to capacity with <u>thousands</u> of <u>houseflies!</u> Presumably, they would be there until such time that it was ready to be used for food. Of course, the carcass would have been thoroughly scoured and cleansed before cooking. If this sounds surprising, - to me, it was!

Houseflies nowadays seem to be less prevalent, thank goodness, but in my boyhood days, they could be a bit of a nuisance in the homes. It was in the days when households hung up sticky "flycatchers" which were a firm paper strip, and inch or so wide, with very sticky surfaces on both sides, and usually after a day or so of hanging, would be covered with dead flies, which, to their misfortune, landed on the sticky surfaces. This was regularly renewed during the warm summer season, - the alternative could be the use of a fly-swatter – like a long handled serving slice, but with a floppy metal spring mesh and to swat them – whenever one felt up to the chase!

Still on the question of meat, in the days before the advent of supermarkets, a town like Kettering would have a scattering of several dozens of private butchers' shops. The local Co-operative Society had a butchery annexed to their many grocery branches, and there were many others in the town centre and quite a number of side streets. All these butchers' shops were clean and well-aired, usually with tiled walls and floors (the latter sprinkled with fresh sawdust). In my boyhood days, I remember sides of fresh beef, mutton and pigs hanging from a metal bar in the shop, also, no doubt, in some back-shop storage areas. From about the mid to late 1930's, we began to see the installation of large metal box-like refrigerators in the corners of the shops, - thereafter the meat began to be stored in them. With the coming of the supermarkets (which pre-packed all fresh meat joints etc.), the individual butchers went into decline, but those remaining could advise about cooking methods, and how to recognise fresh meat, etc.

My last description is a human tale. It is an incident in my life when I was about 12 or 13 years of age. It was Kettering Carnival time, and I, together with many others, filled the footpaths to await the passing-by of a long procession of decorated floats, carnival bands and a host of individual participants. I took my place in Montagu Street near the corner of Wellington Street. There were lots of smiling faces as I looked across the street, but a casual glance among those standing in my vicinity was a young "Mum". I find it difficult to judge the age of such people, but I would guess she would have been in her late teens – 17, 18 or 19 years. She had a pleasant face with smiles as she chatted with her friends. She was standing, and she cuddled a baby as it suckled the mother. The baby's head, together with a shawl draped loosely over hers and the baby's head, kept it a discreet feed. As I was standing only about a couple of feet from this display of mother care, I could make no more than a fleeting glance. In that very brief span of time, I noticed the pale, almost silk-like expanse of her neck, shoulder and chest (which was not immediately needed), but that couple of seconds was enough to emphasise the silken nature of her skin. From her neck, a fine blue vein followed a clear path down here chest until it disappeared behind the top of her dress. I can still visualise it after all these years.

Of recent years (2005/6/7) some people who send letters to newspapers, magazines, etc., have described baby feeding in a public place as disgusting, undignified, etc., which ought to be banned. I believe such people have a wrong opinion – breast-feeding is a <u>perfectly natural act</u>. Mothers who find the need to feed their child would, in their own interest, seek privacy, and by their own prudence, act accordingly. Some traders, - (not a lot), make facilities available for baby feeding, nappy changing, etc., which is a generous act, and a very desirable service, so – about this "unbelievable" act, I say to <u>all</u> the Mums and babies, - good health and happiness!

Narrative 34

SAVOUR THE MOMENT!

Every moment in time has some effect on human emotions. Some for example, are saddening or sorrowful, pleasant, joyous, calming, exciting, mind-boggling, and many others. These have differing impacts and can raise passions in a variety of ways, such as surprise, pride, resignation, fury, excitement, affection, contentment, fervour, enthusiasm, cordiality, thrills, heart-warming, and many more profound and positive thoughts. All these, interspersed with occasional negative thoughts, will register in the mind's retentive cells, but immediately become memories at the completion of each incident or time-span.

All human beings possess the faculty of mustering these occurrences, except the dissolute members of the population, whose minds carry very little except for activities which have an immediate effect of self-gratification, also, of course, (very sadly), those who are ailing from mental illness, or those, for whatever reason have become "loners", and have opted-out of almost all the normal activities encountered by the majority of the population.

So, over the years, anyone with a retentive mind, which can be stimulated with regular usage, - (useful maxim – use it or lose it!), will have gathered a vast assortment of memories over a whole range of circumstances as they occurred. The most outstanding ones will, most probably, be those which had the greatest impact at the time – examples – tragedies of death in the family or close friends, serious accidents, violent weather (floods, snow, storms, drought etc.) There may also be some that haunt a person because of one or two stupid mistakes made which were personally shameful at the time. But there will almost always be a proliferation of more pleasant occasions – excitement, pride, happiness, good holiday memories whenever they are recalled, and that depends on the impact they made at the time they were recorded in the mind.

Certainly, as one gets older, they can become <u>particularly pleasurable</u> memories. So I say, <u>at all times</u> be aware of the many good things encountered during a lifetime, and, as it states on the title of this composition – "Savour the moment" – every one of them <u>quickly</u> becomes a <u>memory!</u>

Narrative 35

"SERVICE" – (WITH A SMILE)

In most spheres of nationwide sporting activities they each have their own descriptive words for the various actions which arise during a game. I offer an example or two:-

CRICKET – "Howzat" (an appeal to the umpire to judge whether or not a batsman is out)

"L.B.W." (Judgement by an umpire of whether a batsman prevented a ball from hitting the wicket with his leg pads)

"No–ball" (A ball judges to be outside the normal bounds for a batsman to reasonably strike it)

FOOTBALL "Hand-ball" (A ball being re-directed by it being touched by hand, or arm, to give some advantage to the perpetrator)

"Off-side" (Judgement by a linesman, or referee, regarding the position of a player at the time the ball reaches them

"Foul" (Any infringement of the rules of the game)

"Free-kick" (A punishment for an infringement which gives some advantage to the opposing team)

"Throw-in" (After the ball passes outside the pitch over the side-line boundary, and awarded to the team not causing it)

RUGBY "Line-out" (Similar to football's "throw-in", but two lines of opposing players attempt to obtain the ball, as it is thrown high over the heads to bringing it back into play

"Tackle" (Any fair stoppage of a player carrying the ball)

"Scrum" (An organised group of opposing players heaving

their shoulders against each other, whilst trying to "hook out" the ball thrown between their feet)

BOXING "Below the belt" (A foul punch judged to have been made to an opponent below the waist)

"Break" (Instruction by the umpire if boxers got so close that they cannot use fists as normal)

GOLF "Fore" (A warning called to spectators or others, who may be in danger of a misjudged ball)

"Tee-off" (The opening hit of a ball to start any new game)

HOCKEY "Bully-off" (The start of a game where two opposing players hit the ground, then each other's sticks three times before hitting the ball into play

TENNIS "Let" (A ball served which hits the top of the net before reaching the opponent's court)

"Fault" (A ball landing over the court lines after a service. Equally if the server's foot is over the line during the serve)

"Service" (This is a warning call to an opponent to indicate the start of a game)

The above mentioned is only a selection of some of the words used in a number of sports. Of course, there are many more, also in many other sports, but this is a precursor to introduce the title of this article.

In the early days of lawn-tennis, it was always played for the fun and excitement also for the benefit of the exercise. In the genteel days, a game was started by one opponent (usually selected by the "toss of a coin") calling "service" to warn the opposing player that it was the signal that scoring was about to start. The modern signal among the professional players of today is by a curt "serve" called by the game's umpire.

A few thoughts on professionalism in almost all sporting activity these days – many people today believe that the sporting and enjoyment elements no longer apply, as almost all of them are conducted as businesses ruled by money and profitability as determined by entrepreneurial pressure. Many of the highly paid players are presented by the media (newspapers, radio and television) as celebrities, not merely for their sporting prowess. Strict rules govern both the participating clubs and individual players, with penalties for wrong-doing in the form of heavy fines or down-grading of status. Destructive actions by players range from irritating vacuous appeals to an umpire or a referee, constant "play-acting" an injury and any way that can interrupt an otherwise free-flowing game. Wrong-doing by clubs and officials are often brought about by underhand dealings. Personalities of players often leave much to be desired, by sulks, long miserable faces, their temperaments and constant disruptive factors. In sports which have much physical contacts between players, some disagreements lead to punching, head-butting etc. All these activities make the games very boring viewing for spectators. Another negative appeal to spectators is, (certainly in the game of tennis), where a player has developed a style of play which relies on almost one main tactic – a strong first service which seldom allows an opponent to make a return hit – sometimes without the ball being touched. It wins points and games, but is a terrible monotony for spectators!

Let us, therefore, regale ourselves with the delight which could be felt at the recognised world-centre for lawn tennis – Wimbledon at the end of the two weeks of contest in the year 2007. British players did not compete well against a plethora of tennis players from around the world. Britain has had no male singles champion since Fred Perry in the 1920's (incidentally I will just mention that in the late 1920's, Fred's father – Mr S.F. Perry, was a Labour Party parliamentary candidate for Kettering - he was not elected!), nor a female singles champion since Virginia Wade nearly 30 years ago. Joy, then, that in 2007 an up-and-rising young male tennis player – Jamie Murray together with his Serbian female partner – Jelena Jarkovic, became the mixed doubles champions, much to the delight and appreciation of those spectators who watched them, and the newspapers' sports correspondents who were enthusiastic with the praise of both of them. Some newspaper descriptions were expressions like "inspired play", "incredible" "emphatic strokes" and very many more! But, the importance to me was the manner in which they played, because a major part of their success were contained in such phrases as "having great fun", "sporting spirit", "laughing and joking" at the end of a series of shots – <u>whether,</u> or <u>not,</u> they <u>won</u> or <u>lost</u> a point! Contrast that with the "<u>grim</u>" and <u>humourless</u> faces of the many professional players, who desire success <u>at all costs!</u>

Certainly, our congratulations can be expressed to our two doubles winners – Jamie and Jelena – it is a shame that there was not a trophy available for <u>happy</u> players, - more's the pity. If there had been, Jamie and Jelena would have <u>won it hand's down!</u>

Narrative 36

KEEP YOUR COOL!

Words often uttered these days are dramatically expressed as <u>global warming.</u> It is given greater credence because it embraces the entire planet and all humanity.

One of the descriptions quoted for illustration, refers to the rapid melting of the present-day giant-sized ice blocks, massed at both North and South poles. Graphic pictures of these are regularly revealed on environmental programmes on the television – large flows of water rushing away from these thawing masses, to add millions of extra gallons to the seas and oceans. This is made more impressive in terms of its effects on rising sea levels, which are set to engulf many miles of coastal areas of many countries and, in some cases, the complete obliteration of some islands in the world. A favourite accusation usually accompanies it, which is to say that some of the blame lies in the activities of mankind, both as individuals, but usually on their way of life.

Some of the progress of the world's living standards, have been brought about by industrial developments, when machinery used by it, involves the emission of toxic gases (popularly referred to as "greenhouse" gases) into the atmosphere. This, it is claimed, has had the effect of polluting the air, which, of course, is essential for the survival of mankind, also for the heating up of ether, (the upper region above the clouds), which surround the earth. A lot of this is blamed onto such things as the fumes from many millions of vehicles in the world, which are reliant on the burning of oil - cars, lorries, coaches etc. As travelling, to many people today, is part of our essential need and desire to travel on every conceivable occasion; this also incorporates air travel, - a heavy user of high octane fuel. Should these facilities become no longer available, it would take away the essence of the life-style of a large body of human activities. Of course, many scientific brains continue to apply their skills to endeavour to discover new methods of locomotion, but, at present their progress cannot be predicted with any accuracy.

There is, I am sure, some justification for saying that the human activities described, do have some contributory effects, on the atmospheric changes, and it should be the responsibility of everyone to play a part in conserving energy by whatever means possible. But, nature itself undergoes extreme cycles! As we think about global warming, a look back in history reveals that the planet has already been subjected to this phenomenon. Surprisingly, fossil remains found in Britain, reveal that it was, at one time, in close proximity to the equator! Fossilised bones of equatorial animals can be found in rocks, and/or the seabed. In fact, the earth's crust has been subjected to a very slow dividing of its solid matter, also to the movement of the tectonic plates lying below the ocean bed. We may remember that a few years ago (probably around 2004AD), these plates overlapped each other under extreme volcanic pressure, and caused massive turbulent and high waves, which flooded some coastal areas in the Far East, and many people were drowned. It was known as a tsunami.

All this land movement has created the continents, countries and islands as we know them today; the earth continues its slow movement, so that, in some cases, it takes hundreds of years before we can detect any dramatic changes in the shape of coast lines.

It may be seen, on a world atlas, that the land masses defined by Africa's western coastline (probably formed at some time millions of years ago) plus the general line of the western Scandinavian coast, together with the west coasts of France and Spain, when compared with the eastern coasts of the U.S.A., and South America, it can be seen that both these coastal shapes (if there was no Atlantic Ocean), would have fitted together (in very general terms) many millions of years ago, but the results of this slow drifting apart of these land masses, has given them their present coastal shapes. All of this presented to us by many experts who have made a great study of these lands and seascapes caused by this enormous movement of land.

It all seems to be a bit like a fantasy, but it is backed up by the fossils and bones found in most unlikely areas of the world, - "Mother Nature" is full of surprises! Another uncanny revelation, which I have only recently read about (June 2007) is that, in the central Congo area of Africa, there is evidence that, due to great climate change there, over just <u>thousands</u> (NOT millions) of years, jungle areas, dense with masses of large trees, undergrowth and a very wide range of insects, large and small animals, snakes, etc., which found these conditions to be favourable, together with the climbing animals and those capable of leaping from branch to branch, and a large range of birds seeking shelter and food (insects, fruit etc.), - these all used this jungle area as their "home territory". As the temperature and other conditions changed over these thousands of years, the jungle gave way to huge areas of grasslands because it became humid, moist and moderate conditions, which were more favourable for the growth needs of grasses, also creatures which could use the long grass as food, nesting and shelter, and they gradually took the place of the previous "tenants". The evidence for this situation is the present pattern of large areas of jungle, in juxtaposition with grassland areas in the Congo area of Africa (until there are any future changes). Just another quirk of nature!

If we find all this to be almost unbelievable, another cycle of extreme change in nature, reveals a time when this country, Britain, was living in an "Ice-age", when little in the way of vegetation could be found, and only a limited number of hardy animals – polar type bears, white hares, etc., were able to survive. After many thousands of years, - another "bolt from the blue" – temperatures changing to warmer conditions, which brought about a gigantic thaw, and voluminous blocks of ice, gradually slid down sloping grounds, and their <u>sheer weight gouged</u> out millions of tons of earth and rocks (most of these very huge), and these were gradually deposited as the thaw was complete. There is much evidence to show that this soil and the rocks ended sometime a hundred or so miles from their original site, and the movement of the soil left many miles of rough valleys. Over the years grasses and vegetation were restored, and many of these newly formed troughs, have become areas of great beauty!

Yes, nature plays some surprising tricks on us! Sometimes in periods of hundreds of years, - sometimes millions, so when we think of climate change today, we <u>can</u> probably detect <u>some</u> kind of change. Another recent example of nature's erratic ways – (in

June 2007) – torrential rain in Britain caused a number of rivers to overflow their banks and, together with the massive rainfall, deeply flooded quite a number of areas, and caused not only a number of lives lost, but many homes and business premises were subjected to flooding. In April of that same year, it was the hottest in recent history. Both of these months belied those which would normally be expected, as illustrated by the well-known maxims - "April showers" and "Flaming June", as a matter of fact, the month of July brought even greater floods due to river banks bursting, and this brought even more life-threatening circumstances. However, if the past "normal" patterns prevail, it will not be in the present generation, nor for generations to come that changes take place. That it <u>will</u> change seems to be inevitable in the long run – that is, if humanity does not first <u>destroy itself!</u> Empires in the past history tell us that mankind can bring about <u>its own downfall or destruction</u> by its irresponsible ways of life – unsuccessful marriages, warring gangs, indiscipline, lack of authority, knives and guns openly carried and too often used in street crime, the breakdown of family life, greed, binge-drinking leading to many quarrels, injuries, hospitalisation, etc., drug-taking (for "kicks") and drug dealing, teenage pregnancies, some "honour" killing of daughters among some of the foreign immigrants according to <u>their</u> way of life, danger from inconsiderate road users, (speeding and dangerous driving), cheating to obtain cash illegally from the social services set up for those in <u>real</u> need, criminal activities of theft, fraud, tax-dodging in the world of commerce, bad parenting (leading to lack of guidance to young members), life threatening sexual diseases, pornography, and <u>many other activities</u> which <u>all</u> have the effect of corrupting a civil way of life.

All these are prohibitive things, in addition to the trauma of surprise attacks by terrorists, as well as global-warming. – <u>Meanwhile, keep your cool!</u>

Narrative 37

<u>OH, NO! - NOT AGAIN?</u>

In this narrative, it is my intention to examine what it means, (to some people), and to talk of "learning the lesson". In national life, we hear the phrase regurgitated so often by various officials – Government Ministers, Chairmen and leaders of industry and others who are in a position with responsibilities. I am sure we have heard the expression on many occasions. Possibly some particular decision did not work out as anticipated, and they attempt to mitigate the circumstances, sometimes with the air of "eating humble pie", but almost always with the promise to learn the lesson, and that, therefore such a mishap would not be repeated!

Some of these unfortunate incidents are of <u>major</u> importance affecting many people, - things like:-

1. Lack of maintenance of dangerous equipment, - a recent case (mid 2007) of a leakage of gas at a gas storage centre. The leakage slowly continued until one or two <u>vast</u> explosions occurred, killing one or two workers, also causing the collapse of a large part of the buildings.

2. A leak of oil at an oil refinery causing a massive fire and loss of life.

3. The loss of life of a dozen or more cockle pickers in Morecambe Bay (in 2005); these were badly organised by "gang" masters. A Government apology followed for failing to control these gang harvesters.

4. The BBC, for showing a film of H.M. The Queen "storming" out of a photographic session "in anger". The real reason was, that the company who prepared the film, <u>altered the sequence</u> of the affair, and the Queen <u>did not</u> "storm out". The BBC "blushed" with the promise to learn the lesson.

5. ITV's "Big Brother" programme, and the company sponsoring it (Endemol), continued baiting those taking part, to be more controversial, causing general grouse by the public; a specific instance – one of the group (Jade), verbally castigated another (Shilpa) because she was "coloured" (Indian). Another apology by the makers who "learned the lesson".

6. A Government department (Agriculture) considerably delayed the E.U. subsidies to the farming communities (because of the introduction of a new system of payment). As at September 2007, payments are <u>not yet</u> paid up to date!

7. Major flooding in many parts of Great Britain due to bad weather (in 2007). The Government (we presume) are still learning the lesson about flood defences. There will probably be more flooding before they have organised this!

8. July/August 2007, - the Government, and private laboratories dealing with cattle foot and mouth outbreak. The apparent reason was probably due to the deterioration of pipe work, between these laboratories, which carried the infectious fluids. There was initial discord between the Government and the private laboratories about <u>who pays</u> for the repairs? They are still "going through the motions" of learning the lesson!

I have only given illustrations of a few examples, but these regularly appear in the daily newspapers – people express their disgust at this foolishness, but, I wonder whether they themselves, have made personal mistakes and vowed – "never again!" If they have done such a thing, I would also wonder – <u>did they</u> do it again?

In this article so far, the comments have referred to activities in the world of high finance, government, etc., but what about individuals? At this point, I give examples of a couple of times in my younger days when I found the lesson learning process to be a useful experience. A family, who lived next door to us, were very friendly. As I was developing into my boyhood stage, the lady of the house fairly regularly held a Christmas party for family and friends. She once said to me "would you like a drink my duck?", and, accepting her offer, I was given half of a small wine glass (probably no more than a desert spoonful) of Port Wine. I drank it, then, within half an hour, I had a fearful headache. I did not associate it with the wine drinking, but on another occasion, I got the invitation to have a similar drink ("don't tell your Mum", said my neighbour host), and the same happened again, - a horrible headache. I still did not associate the drink and headaches, but after just one more time, I determined that red wine gave me the rotten head pains, and I learned the lesson. Once I had established the link, I have never, from that day to the present time had a drink of this kind of wine, in fact, wines of any kind for the same reason.

The second incident which affected me was during the years of the Second World War, - probably around 1942/43. By that time, I had become a commissioned officer of the Royal Marines, and on an evening out, I met up with a couple of Royal Naval Officers, and during our chat, I learned that they were the skipper, and the second officer of an LST (a ship designed to carry military tanks) which was in dry-dock for minor repairs. Their "tipple" was a gin and it (Italian Vermouth), and to keep them company, I did the same. The flavour did not seem to be unpleasant, and turns were taken with several rounds. When they were ready to leave, I did also. I felt quite well until - I stepped out of the door into the fresh air, and, with frightening suddenness, I felt ill, had intense hiccups and a little shaky feeling. I, and they, realised that I would not be able to return to my barracks that evening. Instead, I spent a very restless night aboard the LST, (still with occasional hiccups) and, still felt "under the weather" the next morning. I decided I would return to barracks, and even the following day I did not feel too good. What lessons? – never again! That is how it has remained since that episode! The kind of fate I suffered seems to be so commonplace these days. Young, and old, people seem to binge-drink, and I am sure it must engender some pretty poor feelings (which they call pleasure!), but do they learn the lesson? In far too many cases they do not, and the effects of both alcohol and drugs do not appear to deter them from many repeat performances! These incidents, together with those who use the credit card facilities, never seem to learn by such mishaps. There are far too many tragic cases!

I have only mentioned two or three examples of a personal nature, but throughout life we can continue to learn the best ways of tackling daily problems of all kinds,- relationships, safety issues at work and at home, decision making, financial matters, maintaining good health, and generally making the best of all aspects of life. All these continue to add to our experience, and the mental maturity process. As I have suggested somewhere among my writings, it can be said of an <u>immature adult</u> (and there are some!), that they have <u>not grown up</u>, and their minds still operate at the inexperienced level!

On the question of experience, the dictionary describes it in many ways, such as – the observation of facts, or skill or knowledge gained, comprehension, understanding, and others. Two figures of speech which may be used – "knowing the ropes", "the scales fallen from one's eyes" etc.

So, - live and learn (particularly learn the lessons!).

Narrative 38

FACT OR FICTION?

I am certain that everyone knows the difference between <u>fact</u> and <u>fiction</u>, but I will reinforce this by giving a precise dictionary specification of each one:-

FACT – "something known to have happened, or to be true, or to exist"

FICTION – "a product of the imagination" or "an invented story".

On the other hand, the dictionary description of the phrase "<u>as a matter of fact</u>", states "strictly factual and not imaginative or emotional". However, I think we often <u>misuse</u> the phrase when discussing, or arguing a point of view, because it sometimes does not support any <u>particular</u> fact!

Something that is not intended to be descriptive, but which are meticulously extracted figures, tabulated for industry, commerce, etc., to show such things as the amount of production, profits, or investment made, etc. It is not just in the money making companies, but organisations which spend other peoples' money, so that it can justify the way it has been spent – e.g. International and National governments, local authorities (and all their departments) charities, sporting and musical organisations, particularly for major events such as Olympics, Commonwealth Games, "Top of the Pops" charts, the world explorations, in <u>fact</u>, any organisations which is spending money subscribed by grant or gift, such as British Legion, Age Concern, Oxfam, NSPCC, RSPCA, etc.

I have listed quite a number merely to illustrate, but there are many multi-thousands more, and the officials of each who are responsible for receiving, and allocating the cash involved, are always anxious to ensure that the figures are presented in the most favourable light, and it is at that stage where those scrutinising the details should concentrate and not be misled, - for example – a glass of wine may have the description of being half full or half empty. Both are true, but the descriptive selection is presented according to how it is desired to be interpreted. Percentages and proportions can be misleading. If we think of percentages as part of the statistical fact presentation, it will be seen that 1% of £10,000 is £1,000 and 1% of £100 is £1, so that if wages or salaries are given as percentage increases, the extra amounts received by each is a very large gap between the high and low paid employees. Both the rich and the poor need to eat more or less a similar quantity, although the quality will, no doubt, be higher for the rich. Of course, the rich set lead a more expensive lifestyle, but regular percentages added by each rise over the years, widens the gap between wealth and poverty which creates a good degree of unfairness within society.

Another example of statistics presented to show a better than true situation could possibly be where a company has undergone a poor trading year, figures of this lack-lustre nature will be "softened" by also presenting trade over a number of years of good results, so that it can be said that, whilst the company has had a poor present trading period, trade over the past "X" years has shown a healthy picture.

Another ploy is the avoidance of actual numbers, by saying something has "doubled " in size, - thus 2 increases by 2 and 15 increases by 15 – something doubled from a low starting base brings a poor increase. Also take care to assess another probable deceptive subtlety – the use of words like "better" – (than what?) instead of actual figures. So, beware of how we interpret these factual statistics!

If we apply the fact/fiction classification to human circumstances, we know, as a fact, that we all progress from our birth to fully-fledged adulthood, (and this is influenced by means of example, education, experience, etc.), also the pace at which we gain our reasoning and commonsense faculties. As I stated, factual information often needs some kind of interpretation, and fictional thoughts are widely varied within the population. Age, in years, is a fact, but age in mind is extremely variable. Children, in their early years (say 4-16 years) can state their actual age, but they often believe themselves to be experienced enough to make mature decisions according to their developing maturity, but many of their judgements reveal their inexperience. Much evidence of this can be seen in their early life choice of friends whom, they are sure will be good, but after some petty squabble, can quickly be ended, then, after a short "cooling-off" period, they become friendly again. When they reach their teenage years, this is very much in evidence between male and female friendships. It becomes a more serious issue after a marriage has taken place, and more so, if there area any children born of the partnership. The adults may be able to withstand the trauma, but it leaves a dreadful confusion for the children.

Final thoughts of this essay are to consider how older peoples' minds may cope with fiction, fantasy, imagination, etc.; - some people have a more imaginative mind than others. Reminding ourselves again about words associated with it, - fancy idealism, inspiration, dreaming, reverie, whimsical, caprice, faddy, - plus many more. It is a fact that ageing comes to us all in due time, and because of it, our physique changes, - bones, muscles, skin, etc., and this confronts people in various ways. Males, if they were once regarded as athletic, vigorous, energetic, toned up, etc., will find many changes with age. All the physical attributes once enabled them to appear smart and manly, and even, in some cases jaunty, stylish, etc. These features fade with age, but a man can still dress well, maintain a good standard of cleanliness, and have good taste.

The effects on females also vary, and their taste, clothes, looks etc., also undergo this changing pattern. Grace and elegance of their younger days can continue in later life, but, like males if there is deterioration of body shape, skin etc., particularly due to the stresses of their body due to child-bearing, and the many years of the body's cyclical preparation for such an event! In their younger days, they may have used cosmetics, - face cream, powder, lipstick, etc. These can still be used at the older age, but it must be remembered that youthful skin is firm, but soft. Ageing skin may become more flabby, with possible signs of the onset of wrinkles. Cosmetics may assist in keeping a certain amount of suppleness, but overuse may lead to the undignified label of "mutton dressed up as lamb!" Grace and elegance does not need the assistance of heavy make-up. Choice of suitable dresses, tops and skirts for the older generation, will certainly maintain a stylish air!

Some elders, especially the ladies, are more and more following the pattern set in the U.S.A. of body surgery and liposuction to firm up any flabbiness, also the use of Botox injections to eliminate a degree of wrinkling, but there can be dangers in this. Everyone will make their won choices, and there are many clinics offering such services. Once again, remember that when they offer an opinion of whether such treatment is suitable for your own particular circumstances, <u>some</u> clinics will be more persuasive for you to undergo the treatment, - to advise otherwise, it will be a <u>loss</u> of business! – Seek advice first from your own doctor or hospital specialist.

Both men and women, at whatever age, will find it beneficial to have a <u>friendly</u> conversational style, as this is usually reciprocated by others, and makes for a more congenial existence, and that <u>is a fact</u>, not <u>fiction!</u>

Narrative 39

YULE-TIDE JOYS

I chose the title YULE for this essay as referring to both Christmas and Yule-tide, the latter being an old-use word (according to a dictionary description) to represent the Christmas Festive Spirit.

Today, this sociable period has changed enormously in my lifetime. A great bearing on this is the huge increase in the wealth of the population due to inflation between my own boyhood days and the present time, (when I am approaching the age of 89). Another factor is in the nature of the much larger national or international traders, and their method of sales promotions, to be found in cities and towns, which directs their selling towards the more expensive goods, rather than the small gift items which could have been purchased from many small retailers of earlier years. That, coupled with the volume growth of technology relating to communications equipment of every conceivable kind (and these still keep developing at a phenomenal pace!)

Children of "working class" parents, expected little (which was what they got!). apart from some kind of maia gift – probably a toy of some sort together with "stocking filler" items – such things as an orange or apple, a small quantity of nuts, and possibly a few sweets or a bar of chocolate.

Today, pressure is applied by larger retail groups (or, nowadays, by internet sales or savings clubs, etc.), so that by the end of the summer holiday period – September/October,- the time for buying Christmas gifts is well under way. One hears of parents who spend hundreds of pounds (sterling) or more on gifts for their children, which seems to be an indication that the country's standard of living has increased considerably.

It is good that today's children have access (and for their own use) to computers etc., which are also part of the regular equipment used by schools. The possible drawback to this is that their use at home does not necessarily pursue the same knowledgeable subjects, and the novelty of a freedom of choice, adds to the fascination of some of the young ones as they search the internet for contacts from almost anywhere world wide, and find it to be somewhat intriguing. They can chat with complete strangers and view things like blogs, chat-lines, pornography, etc. Contacts of this sort can spell danger as some "chatting" strangers encourage the possibility of them becoming more closely acquainted, and sometimes to the point where there is an agreement to meet. It can sound exciting, but without the experience of understanding the hazards of such associations, some young people actually leave home to pursue the adventure, sometimes with tragic results. Such activities as these seem more commonplace today, as young children and teenagers believe they know enough about life and that everything will work out to their advantage. The attitudes of both young and old has completely changed. It does not need much searching in newspapers and news bulletins to learn of the great horrors which arise from these tangled liaisons when some young ones, particularly young females, are groomed and trafficked into prostitution to anywhere in the world – a completely loathsome abomination to responsible people.

There is, I believe, a powerful influence to be found within religious orders. There are many differing faiths, and whilst there is no perfection, individuals who have a faith, particularly a Christian faith, strive for perfection by its influence. A Christian believer looks upon Christmas as a celebration to honour Jesus Christ – their Prince of Peace.

May our minds ponder on such an effect if it became a universal pursuit!

Narrative 40

<u>THE EPOCH OF PLASTICS</u>

Even a quick glance through historical records will reveal a list of inventors who, by their talent and skills have devised numerous commodities and great technologies of major importance for all mankind, and they cover a whole string of benefits and techniques for use in the worlds of industry, science, fashion, transport and other general needs of life. One such invention saw the light of day in the U.S.A. in 1937. It concerned the business of fashion, - namely nylon, an oil-based yarn which to a large degree, superseded the natural fibre – silk! It achieved world acclamation, particularly by the ladies, when nylon stockings were produced! This product, however, has <u>no connection</u> with another oil-based material, except that they were <u>both synthetics,</u> that is <u>manufactured</u> rather than a <u>natural</u> product. It's name – <u>PLASTIC</u>, but, not being a fashion item, it did not, at first, get the same fanfare of excitement, because it was not until the years that followed that its <u>versatility</u> was realised.

In its early days, it was mainly produced and used in sheet form as a packaging material, but once discovered, many other scientific brains began experimenting and producing it in a deluge of other forms. Being impervious to water, it began to take the place of rubber for a variety of rainwear, both light-weight or of heavier densities. It was also used for Wellington boots and for other footwear components, - uppers, soles, heels, etc. The properties of plastic seem to be almost endless, and the following are some of them so far discovered.

1. Waterproof (as already stated)
2. Can be either transparent or opaque
3. It is mouldable, from small to large shapes and sizes in infinite forms
4. Can be a clear or a magnifying sheet
5. Can be in a flexible form with a degree of elasticity

6. Can be made very strong and durable (used for tyres on prams, wheelchairs – <u>not</u> heavy vehicles
7. Can be of a brittle nature (boxes caskets etc.)
8. Can be made heat-resistant (useful for microwave or oven cooking)
9. It can retain its permanence – almost indefinitely (both above and below ground)
10. <u>Can</u> be made bio-degradable (e.g. fragmented into small flakes after a certain period of time)
11. It can be bonded onto fabrics (e.g. furniture covering)
12. Can be both strong and stretchy (carrier bags, etc.)
13. Resists dirt, dust and germ penetration

Before I proceed to proclaim the qualities of plastics any further, I would like to remind anyone who remembers the introduction of plastic, of the way in which one company used and proclaimed its worth. This company traded in the U.S.A – its name "TUPPERWARE" which produced a range of domestic boxes, basins, jars, etc., made from a strong, but flexible gauge of plastic, moulded into these various containers, with a lid which fitted tightly to make it airtight, and, they said, would "last a lifetime". Their selling method was novel. Persuading various, and many, housewives to invite friends to a "party", during which, the various Tupperware articles were displayed, and many sold! They were referred to as "Tupperware Parties". Such was the success, that many other traders adopted the same method for such things as jewellery, lingerie, cosmetics, etc.

Tupperware was a registered trade-mark, but similar containers were made by other companies, and became well used as children's lunch boxes, picnic packaging etc. They are not used on the same wide scale, but, many Tupperware articles can <u>still</u> be found in use, four decades from their introduction.

Plastics can be found over a very wide range of domestic and commercial use, - a few examples of what materials they substitute, over a wide circle of users.

1. <u>Domestic</u> – bowls, basins, dishes, food storage, also cooking, bottles (glass), some children's toys (including dice/dominoes), write on/wipe off memo pads.
2. <u>Grocery</u> items - cartons, bottles, jars, pre-packed items.

3. <u>Medical/Dental</u> – various fluid tubes (blood, water, urine, etc.), casing for many items of equipment (syringes, hospital mattress covers, drip-bags (catheters).

4. <u>Personal hygiene</u> – combs, backing for bristle brushes, toothbrushes, <u>large</u> baths, bowls, razor handles etc.

5. <u>Gardening</u> – (self +professional) – plant pots, seed trays, handles for many tools (mowers, rakes, dibbers, secateurs, hedge-clippers, edge cutters etc.

6. <u>Hairdressing</u> – (self + professional) – curlers, slides, protective "bibs" and sheets, rinsing-water funnel guides

7. <u>Office work</u> – casings for much equipment (computers, typewriters, filing cabinets, etc.) protective envelopes for a wide range for paperwork, also casing for pens, markers etc.

8. <u>Civil engineering</u> – large scale underground reinforced heavy tubing

9. <u>General Household</u> – wheelie bins/boxes, bin liners, dustpans and brushes, handles(vice bone and ivory) for knives, forks, spoons – disposable picnic ware, knives, forks, plates, beakers etc.

10. <u>Agriculture</u> – great use of poly tunnels, rainproof covers for stacks

11. <u>Architects</u> – set squares, "T" squares, protractors, measuring straight edges, drawing boards, etc.

12. <u>Vehicles</u> – fabricated seat covers, accessories like mirror-backing, disc holders, instrument panels, glove compartments, etc.

13. <u>Fashion</u> - shop display units, coat hangers, display models footwear components, etc.

14. <u>General</u> – roofing, ceiling tiles, cowling, awnings, vice tarpaulins, emergency shelters, groundsheets, mock shell, table cloths, and a large variety of other uses.

The above are, by no means a complete tally and new discoveries <u>keep adding</u> to the list.

It is, by <u>any</u> standard of judgement a bewildering, mind-boggling catalogue of its application. I would personally say – hail to this <u>wonder synthetic</u>!

Narrative 41

<u>WHAT'S –A-NAME !</u>

Occasionally, one may hear the expression during police enquiries, "someone known as", - followed by a name and this sums up the need for having individual names. From the dim and distant past, people in tribal, racial clan or caste groups, have been identified by being given some kind of fraternal identity. The aim of this narrative is to refer to various links associated with that nomenclature.

There is such a wide variety of names, and a great deal of time could be spent discovering their origins, but without attempting to delve into it in such great depth, I offer a few thoughts on the subject. It can be seen that some names have direct connections. <u>First</u> names such as Jack, Tim and John, gave rise to Jackson, Timson and Johnson as <u>family</u> names via their offspring's – sons of Jack, Tim and John. There are also many others derived in the same way. There are many hundreds of other family names, by whatever means they were chosen. These were once commonly referred to as <u>Christian,</u> or <u>Baptismal</u> names instead of <u>first</u> names, and the <u>surname</u> instead of <u>family</u> names. Christian names are sometimes given to a new born baby according to what happens to be popular at the time. Names like Emma, Amy and Eva, could be commonly heard in the latter part of the 19th Century, then, after falling out of favour for a while, they re-appeared from about the mid to late 20th Century, and are still quite popular in the early 21st Century. Similarly, boys' names like George and Charlie, which still often appear in the early 21st Century.

The <u>source</u> of names may provoke some interesting thoughts. The following tabulation of both Christian and surnames indicate how the identities came about. It is just a <u>small</u> selection as examples:-

DERIVATION OF SOME CHRISTIAN AND SURNAMES

SURNAMES

SOURCE	NAME	SOURCE	NAME
TRADES	POTTER	PURSUITS	WALKER
	PAINTER		RIDER
	BAKER		TROTTER
FOOD	SALT	BIRDS	PEACOCK
	PEPPER		DUCK
	BEAN		EAGLE
COLOURS	BLACK	BUILDINGS	HOUSE
	WHITE		CASTLE
	PINK		HALL
ENVIRONMENT	BUSH	GEOGRAPHIC	FROST
	CAVE		SNOW
	HILL		WATERS
	MOSS		
ANIMALS	MUTTON		
	LAMB		
	BACON		

CHRISTIAN NAMES

SOURCE	NAME	SOURCE	NAME
FLORAL	HEATHER	JEWELS	RUBY
	POPPY		PEARL
	ROSE		BERYL
	LILY		
	FERN		
	DAISY		
	HOLLY		
	IVY		

HAZEL

The lists illustrate the probable source of some names in frequent use, and I am sure that you may be able to add more; however there are many more that use "pet" names such as "Fluff", "Muz", "Squigy", and hundreds more. Surnames like White, Clark and Miller, are sometimes prefixed with "Pinky" "Nobby" and "Dusty" (respectively) by their friends.

We can come across hyphenated surnames – sometimes called "double-barrelled". Upon marriage, the female may not wish to give up her maiden name completely, and wishes to have it conjoined with that of her husband, to make any combination such as Allison-Cooper, Lawrence-Jones, etc., and this (or any other name change) can be made by Deed- Poll. In regard to name changes, there have been cases of a criminal nature, where, sometimes a name change is to obliterate a reference to the original <u>real</u> name. It is, I believe, a complicated process, but the criminal will search for the details of an untimely death of any person whose description can appear to apply to them. They obtain the birth certificate of that person and thereafter their real name "disappears" from use!

When some new name has been popularised by some film actor/actress, or others in, say, the musical "pop" business, parents of a new-born child, are tempted to give the name to their off-spring – names like Kylie, Britney,(girls') Clark, Casey, (boys'), etc. Incidentally, I have just seen a published newspaper poll (Dec. 2007), of the top 5 boys' and girls' names, - they are:

<u>Boys'</u>   Jack, Thomas, Oliver, Joshua, Harry

<u>Girls'</u>   Grace, Ruby, Olivia, Emily, Jessica.

Note: - many of them are well used names from the past.

Various film actors/actresses give themselves "stage names", for example – American "cowboy" actor, John Wayne, had the Christian and surname of Michael Marion Morrison. The suave

Bristol-UK actor Carey Grant was originally named Alexander Archibald ("Archie") Leach. American actress Marilyn Monroe's original names were Norma Jean Mortenson. One other British comedian – Stan Laurel, - (Laurel and Hardy fame) I think, (and here I am completely relying on my memory!) once had the surname of Jefferson. There are, of course, hundreds of others!

Having had a lot of probing thoughts about names, I have sometimes wondered <u>how</u> many nick-names were selected, - the mind "boggles!" However I will mention just one which I know is true. A new teacher commenced at my secondary school (approx. 1931/2), and on his very first day, two or three pupils were chatting in the playground at break-time, and, of course, the topic of thought was –"What do you think about him?" Comments were quite favourable and one of the group (of which I was part), said "He looks well dressed – a brand new suit, and a "posh" new shirt, (the material of which was woven in small squares), - "a bit like a draught -board" Immediately one of the group (I believe his name was Brookes), made an "off the cuff" remark – "It's got to be <u>draughty</u>!" Within hours of its inception, I would imagine the <u>complete</u> school population of girls and boys became fully aware of it, and the man, a good teacher, was thereafter referred to as "draughty".

I am sure there are many more things that could be unearthed about names, but this article may set minds thinking upon it (that's if you have time to spare, - what's-a-name!!)

Narrative 42

I'M A DREAMER!

There was an old song which had the words "I'm a dreamer, - aren't we all?" – and many dreams reveal a wide variety of involuntary thoughts, - many on subjects which we rarely think about, and are sometimes almost impossibilities for a human brain to even contemplate. I occasionally find such fanciful thoughts passing through my mind before I finally fall asleep at night-time (a kind of subliminal day-dream), the variety of subjects is almost unimaginable, but an unusual one occurred to me in late December 2007, and it must have been over a couple of hours in duration before I finally went to sleep! I do not know why it should have arisen, because I have been retired from work for <u>over 23 years,</u> but the subject was about "setting up a new business!" – an unlikely subject at my age – (at that time, within three months of reaching my 89th birthday!)

The following morning, I found the subject <u>still</u> very strongly on my mind, and whilst it would never apply to me, by recalling it, (in this composition now), may make you wonder why it should have even entered my head! I had <u>no idea</u> of what sort of business it might be, but, whatever it was, there were a multiplicity of thoughts and actions which need consideration before <u>any</u> type of business is commenced. A popular idea of gathering many thoughts, (usually from a sizeable group of people), is what is known as "brainstorming" – of American origins, - and the idea is to quickly gather <u>spontaneous</u> thoughts from everyone present, and from the list of ideas, it is followed by a discussion about their relevance and importance. From this, a finalised list of ideas, old or new would be made of those that would produce a good line of action which may prove fruitful. Without the help of an assemblage of minds, recording their thoughts, in a <u>personal</u> fantasy dream, my mind became very activated, and the following list will reveal the reason for the duration of it, - at least a couple of <u>turbulent</u> hours, -(only a selection is offered,- I cannot recall them all).

MY BRIEF "BLITZ"OF THOUGHTS - Do I really <u>want</u> to start a business? What kind of goods/services? Are my goods/skills of a good enough standard? Any desires for further expansion? Where would the premises be located? How would I let the public know? Have I got sufficient capital? Am I ready for long hours of work in the early days? Do I know the laws relative to trading? Do I need insurance cover, - if so, for what? Are there any Government regulations which must be recognised? Am I conversant with the way of establishing a suitable price for my goods? – (bearing in mind competitors' prices). Could I get access to further capital, if it was necessary? – (bearing in mind that <u>"ploughed back"</u> profit is the <u>cheapest</u> form of capital). Am I aware of the suppliers of goods? Do I need any kind of transport? Are the premises large enough to allow vehicles both access and garaging? Do I need professional help with Annual Accounts and Balance Sheet? Are there regulations about annual accounts? Am I capable of understanding the P.A.Y.E. system and regular payment to Government submitted? Do I understand the "Conditions of Service" legislation? How would any extra labour be trained? Do I realise that capital would be required for a long time, before any profit comes from it? Do I realise that without adequate capital, trading would have to cease? Are Banks/ friends/relatives a suitable source to raise any extra capital needed? Would I trade as a sole-trader (one-man business), partnership or as a limited liability company? Do I realise the significance of each of them? Do I realise the importance of insuring the business, and if so, what would need to be covered?

The above list is just the <u>"tip of an iceberg"</u> selection of my transient thoughts, although I know that there needs to be <u>many, many</u> more!

From this "personal brainstorm" list, I found my night time fantasy continuing next by categorising them under suitable headings like "Premises", "Suppliers", "Government Regulations", "Transport needs", "Insurance cover", "Finances/Accounts" etc., etc. I then put these headed lists into some kind of sequence of priority for procedure and from that, some type of plan of action might then be possible, and a basis of business could emerge.

As I remarked, these thoughts were "off the cuff", but some study of business text books will, without doubt, be very desirable. In fact my "fantasy" included the possibility of employing other people, and I even went through the method by which they might be assessed, by producing a draft "application form" which would probe things like – punctuality, temperament, the will and wish to work etc. What an "ogre" I appeared to have become! I do not really believe that such harsh action would ever be my <u>real</u> mode; - the mind plays some funny tricks!

You will have deduced from that brief description, why it took me such a long time before I settled down for a sleep, - I suppose it helps to keep the mind active!

<u>PS</u>. I had a very comfortable and restful night's sleep once I "dropped off!"

Narrative 43

<u>WHO ARE YOU?</u>

In one of my earlier compositions entitled "What's-a-name" I described how individuals are distinctively identified as personal and unique beings, by the use of their first names, family names, pet names, nick-names, etc., and I did so in a <u>light-hearted</u> manner, but in this article, the use of names, is treated more seriously, as they are continually being used in most walks of life, for <u>many</u> reasons.

A profusion of peoples' records are already held by various organisations for their own benefit. These are a diverse mixture of records, - some <u>governmental,</u> and endless others by <u>private</u> and <u>commercial</u> organisations. A selection of examples is as follows:-

1. <u>Medical records</u> held by G.P.'s, showing the types and dates of illnesses, drugs and other medications prescribed and the duration of their use, etc. Also recommendations for specialist treatment when considered necessary, with the results of various health checks given and recorded. There will be the circumstances leading to the need for care services, etc. All this information needs complete privacy, although it sometimes seems that having certain illnesses, - heart, lungs, bowels, osteoporosis, diabetes, etc. etc., "mysteriously" reaches the ears of companies which then bombard selected persons with literature and "special" offers and cures for such ailments.

2. <u>Hospital records</u> of all appointments at the hospital, all visits for tests, X-rays, surgery, accident and emergency treatments, also any follow-up appointments. As with medical records, they also <u>seem</u> to get known by many drug companies, also, importantly, insurance companies, which are keen to know the probable longevity of certain illnesses.

3. <u>Chemists</u> record all prescriptions issued, and the repeat requests.
4. <u>Dental and Ophthalmic</u> records are kept, and they are sometimes very useful for <u>identifying</u> a person who is confused – loss of memory etc.
5. <u>Legal records</u> – any misconduct which proceeds through either lower or higher County Courts and High Courts are recorded and available for perusal in any subsequent occurrences – Fines levied for any crimes and any compensations paid.
6. <u>Care organisations</u> – Warden controlled or Nursing and Residential Homes, both national and private, maintain records for any future reference – including any spells in hospital etc.
7. <u>Social allowances</u> both government and private, which are made to help to pay for services needed.
8. <u>Local Authority</u> records maintained regarding rates levied and paid, also concessions where appropriate. The type of housing, either rented or owned, also requests for planning permission to allow alterations to the property. Sometimes it may upgrade the Band of values which determine rates to be paid. A tally is kept of late or <u>non</u> payments in regard to all taxes due.
9. <u>Taxation</u>
   a) <u>Income Tax</u> – records maintained over many years.
   b) <u>Benefits paid</u> – records maintained over many years.
   c) <u>Requests and Reasons</u> to seek extra benefits.
   d) <u>Unemployment payments</u> (including Job-seekers allowances)
   e) <u>Industrial injuries</u> allowances(may become Disablement Benefit over the course of time)
   f) <u>Birth and Family Allowances</u> N.B. All births <u>must</u> be registered.
   g) <u>Housing benefits</u> where appropriate – records held.
10. <u>Banks and Building Societies</u> record of Current Accounts, Savings and Investment Accounts, etc., Banks issue PIN (Personal Identity Number) for all their customers. This

number is <u>strictly private</u> to the customer, who is responsible for their safety.

11. <u>Immigration details</u> and (if known) their addresses (or point of contact), also employment, and any allowances paid to them, etc.

12. <u>Private Traders</u> – Supermarkets or small businesses – records of all transactions other than cash payments (till receipt valid for a limited period). Particularly, a <u>perpetual</u> record is kept of all bad debts which brings difficulty or refusal of any request for further credit.

13. <u>Internet trading</u> Courts can demand information of any illegal trade.

14. <u>Petty thefts</u> from shops etc. Groups of traders often set up a chain of shops to keep each other informed of possible trouble.

15. <u>Passport Identity</u> – the need for a permit to travel overseas, with the cost borne by the applicant. Requires periodic renewal.

16. <u>Vehicle Records</u> D.V.L.A (Government Agency) maintains records of all vehicle sales, and certification of any which are no longer used on the country's roads. Also M.O.T details, mileages etc. There is cooperation with the Police to locate car thefts, or those ignoring speed cameras etc.

17. <u>Motor Vehicle Road Tax and Insurance</u> – compulsory in both cases (cooperation with DVLA when required).

18. <u>Other Miscellaneous Groups</u> Shared ownership in Industry, Commerce (via Stock Exchange) Annuity Insurances (<u>not</u> Index Linked), National Savings Bonds, ISA/PEP/ INVESTMENT BOND FUNDS – recorded and controlled via Building Societies and Investment Fund companies.

It will be realised from the list of funds and authorities given (there are probably others not included), but they are important and that <u>we, the public</u>, are <u>subject to the dictates of many strict regulations,</u> and these controls we have grown up to accept as being reasonably appropriate (no doubt with a degree of aggressive grumbling!), but they are important because they govern our activities, particularly over matters concerning the handling and transfer of monetary matters.

At the beginning of the Second World War (1939-45), all the UK population were issued with an official Identity Card (pale blue) and about half the size of a postcard. I am pretty sure we did not believe that any German personnel would have been deterred from arriving in Britain without suitable identity information, but the cards were helpful, to a degree, in ensuring that our various entitlements were provided. It did seem to be a "crumb of comfort" it offered by the feeling that we were one nation working together to oppose the Nazi enemy! It was issued free of any costs to all citizens (no costly modern technology involved) and, one might say "it served its purpose".

There is talk today (early 2008) of the need for the nation to have individual Identity Cards issued to all citizens – these of course, would be produced using up to date technology (including facial "scans", eye colouring etc.), and (it seems to me), that they would prove useful for dealing with many aspects of today's "tangle of needs" (as listed) or whenever any form of identity is required. Critics of such a scheme will say that they would achieve nothing worthwhile. Many of these complainants raise their voices on all sorts of issues – they are referred to as the guardians of "Civil Liberties". They seem to be vociferous against many (usually Government) policies which, they claim, is denying freedom of action. My belief is that we, the citizens of the United Kingdom, enjoy considerably more freedoms than many, or most, other world countries!

One legitimate claim against them being made a legal requirement is the fact that citizens would have to "pay for the privilege" of owning one! That, I believe, would be an "administrative disaster". Payment for them would have to be collected and acknowledged individually, - (a costly administrative problem). How would non-payers be dealt with? If they refuse, what kind of punishment would be made, - a fine? (this might also remain unpaid!) – a community service? (costly in terms of the huge problem of training of sufficient and suitable custodians, also the kind of duties to be undertaken); - short or medium gaol term? – all very costly for the taxpayers to "foot the bill"!

Would payment be demanded from immigrants? (against whom much of the identification would be needed) – they would probably only be able to pay with allowances paid to them by the British Government (e.g. taxpayers!) Critics, again, might, justifiably, say that <u>security of important</u> information is at risk, following recent losses of important details from the Dept. of Works and Pensions (on two discs containing private details of millions of citizens!), also one or two more important losses from Government Departments, including the DVLA. These are <u>scandalous</u> and must <u>never happen again</u>, particularly if details of Identity Card information went astray! There would need to be a <u>complete certainty</u> for their security, handling and transference of any information between persons who are permitted access to them, between departments (Government or any other <u>authorised unit</u>), which request to see them (e.g. by a very senior authorised figure). In such cases, I believe that there <u>must be a check</u> by at least <u>two senior</u> responsible persons (probably each holding <u>one</u> of <u>two</u> differing key necessary to open a safe in which documents are stored, - <u>both keys</u> being <u>needed</u> for each transaction, also their responsibility for the follow up of their safe return after perusal. It ought not to be beyond the wit of men (or women) to devise such a system, with severe punishments (even dismissal) for <u>any</u> official who digresses!

The wheels of Government turn <u>very</u> slowly, and it will be doubtful whether I will live long enough to see such a system installed (that is, - if they bother!), but I fully approve of it being established.

The latest report which I read, as coming from the Prime Minister, Gordon Brown in January 2008, states that nobody should fear the introduction of Identity Cards, - they are designed for use by the immigrant population (it does not say "<u>initially</u> by them"), but if it did commence in that way, I feel fairly sure that it would be fully enforced by <u>gradual submission</u> to eventually include all citizens!

P.S. I would not personally object if <u>any</u> details of <u>my life</u> were recorded. I like <u>most</u> others, <u>respect the laws and regulations</u> of this country, and I make a <u>conscious</u> effort to abide by them! They have been set up by the democratic process (not <u>always</u> perfect!) and <u>not</u> by a <u>dictatorial leader</u>, or <u>system</u>, of Government!

Narrative 44

SOME SILENT "ACTION" MOVIES

(Early/Mid 1920's)

Many early comedy men of the films, - such names as Larry Semon, Edgar Kennedy, Charlie Chaplin, Buster Keaton, Keystone Kops, Harold Lloyd, and others, all became very well known. Many of their acts were of the "slap-stick" variety – very much "knock-about" action, and the following scenarios are a few of them which were often witnessed.

1. Falls from great heights (onto a thick bed of straw, or similar) – even so they were dangerous to perform.
2. Hanging by the fingertips from a window ledge – (having had the ladder knocked away after they had climbed to the top).
3. "Accidental" falls into a bath of water, lake or swimming pool (usually with a final mouthful "squirted" from their mouth).
4. (Harold Lloyd) – walking along narrow girders on the top part of a partially built sky-scraper – often with "mock-misfooting" a number of times.
5. (Buster Keaton) – famous scene, - the collapse of a large wooden shed, - one side at a time, - with the door or window frame on each of the sides crashing – <u>exactly</u> – to ensure that each frame fell <u>over</u> Buster as he stood (without a blink) until the complete building lay flat on the ground around him. N.B. He did such things as a real <u>live</u> performance. If it was miscalculated, he could have been killed, or seriously injured!
6. (Buster Keaton) – running fast down a steep hillside as a mass of very <u>heavy</u> boulders, and a mass of smaller ones, closely followed him (dangerously closely), the whole way

down. Incidentally, whatever situation he found himself in – funny or serious, - he never smiled!

7. (Harold Lloyd), another famous scene – hanging to the hands of a clock face, high up on a tall building. <u>N.B</u>. Whilst the filming angles enhanced the "danger" by judicious placing of the cameras, nevertheless, both he, and Buster ran many risks whilst filming their actions.

8. (Charlie Chaplin) – ducking and diving, as he was being chased by the "Kops". Lots of his portrayals had <u>"pathos"</u> in their story line.

9. (The Keystone Kops) – a group of uniformed American police, with their motor-wagon, chasing after criminals, with arms akimbo, and legs constantly spreading wide as they jumped about, and this added to the excitement.

Incidentally, all the situations I have mentioned so far, were greatly enhanced to exaggerate the scenes, because these early films were shot by hand cameras at a slow rate, so that when they were projected at the normal speed, all the actions shown on the cinema screen, moved at a <u>very fast rate</u>, which added to the fascination.

There were <u>many more</u> of these early American comedy stars, and the Hollywood film studios turned them out at a rapid rate.

10. (Laurel and Hardy) – the well known partners, relied, in the main, for a normal speed of action, but over the many years, managed to originate a mass of funny scenes. I will mention one or two.

(a) Laurel and Hardy walking along together, and Laurel, unaware of what had happened, turned, with surprise, to see that Hardy was not still with him. He looked behind him, tentatively a couple of times before he realised that Hardy was some way away, lying prostate on the pathway (sidewalk) with one leg down an open inspection cover.

(b) The couple walking through swing doors had one walking one way and one pushing the door the opposite way, result – both walked into the doors, with the inevitable "bonk on the conk".

(c) Hardy often complained that Laurel had "gotten him into another fine mess!" (which he did many times).

(d) I have lost count of the number of times when one of them removed the other's bowler hat, so that a clout on the head could be administered.

(e) A deliberate jabbing of a finger into the other's eye, with the inevitable "Aaargh!" from the one receiving it.

(f) One scene I well remember, was in the early days of the motor-car, - (the Ford "Tin-Lizzie"), where the car had rattled to a shuddering halt, and as they both sat there, one car door dropped off, followed by a second one, and finally the other two doors, and, as they sat there with a surprised look on their faces, the final doom and insult was the collapse of the four wheels and the pair still sat there with a very frozen deadpan look, with one still holding on to the steering wheel!

(g) Another occasion with these early model cars, they thought they could drive through a shallow water-crossing, but as they drove into it, the car went deeper and deeper, until it was completely immersed, leaving two bowler hatted couple with just their head and shoulders above the water!
There were quite a number of other comical characters, each with their own particular style of presentation, but, for me, they were exciting times.

As these developments took place, some American artists conceived the possibility of the movement of cartoon figures on the screen. They experimented with a series of cartoon characters, and with each succeeding sketch making slight movements recorded a succession of sketches, so that, when projected at the normal speed, the figures shown on the screen appeared to move, - this principle was seen in a later form by a series of photographs depicting action when shown in quick successions (e.g. the sea-side pier peep-shows (the bioscope) such as "what the butler saw" sketches etc.)

The earliest of these (from my memory) were the two characters, Mutt and Jeff, - they were depicted as two smallish male figures, and their activities were confined to simple movements, - walking, running, jumping, chasing after a ball or a hat, leapfrogging, waving a flag, etc. They emerged from about the mid 1920's.

The painters continued to experiment with another cartoon "star", - this time a dog! They christened it <u>Felix</u>, and for the next year or so became quite popular. Filmgoers became fascinated enough to have a short musical lyric written, - the rhyme – "Felix keeps on walking". Felix was often depicted as walking on his two hind legs, with his front paws behind his back. I remember the tune and most of the words which were:

Felix keeps on walking, keeps on walking still,

With his hands behind him, you will always find him,

He walks the streets with weary plod, but finds no mice to
thrill.

Felix keeps on walking, keeps on walking still.

By the time Felix became established, another American artist – Walt Disney, invented another cartoon, - <u>Mickey and Minnie Mouse</u>, with one or two other animal pets.

Again, initially shown as a black/white cartoon, but it wasn't too long (about the later 1920's/early 1930's), before Mickey & Minnie Mouse appeared <u>in colour</u>. They became very popular. Disney himself was very enterprising, and turned some of them into 60/90 minute length main film presentations. Also invented was another cartoon couple – <u>TOM & JERRY</u>, which became probably, more popular than Mickey Mouse.

Disney also transformed many well known Fairy stories into long main films, in colour, and excellent musical sound tracks – "Snow White and the Seven Dwarfs", "Peter Pan", "Pinocchio", etc.- all highly successful. He also produced a number of historical sagas of excellent quality. There were a number of other cartoon type films in circulation, probably not so well known as the ones mentioned, but among those, it is certainly important to mention one, as it had a good period of popularity, that name – <u>"Popeye the Sailor"</u>.

I remember this period of the silent movies with great pleasure. It was certainly no perfection, as the film was a celluloid strip, which became very scratched as it passed through projectors s often, and did not allow a clear picture at times (but good enough to entertain), also quite a number of stoppages because the brittle film had snapped, causing short breakdowns, until it was repaired, - cinematography was still in its infancy! It became a great influence on both the young ones, of which I was part, also to many mature adults; - evidence of this could be seen in the <u>long</u> queues outside <u>all the cinemas,</u> as the patrons waited patiently for their turn to see this new kind of entertainment at their disposal.

It was certainly a stimulating time!